Mission Hope

VOLUME 3

The Power of Love

Mission Hope

VOLUME 3

The Power of Love

Printed and Electronic Versions
ISBN Paperback 978-1-956353-56-3
ISBN eBook:978-1-956353-57-0
(Char Murphy / Motivation Champs)

The book was printed
in the United States of America.

To order additional copies or bulk order contact the publisher,
Motivation Champs Publishing.
www.motivationchamps.com

Contents

Foreword

Being deeply loved by someone gives you strength, while loving someone deeply gives you courage. —Lao Tzu

Love is such a powerful word, and it has a way of being an intimate part of our daily life. Whether we know it or not, there is an innate part of us always seeking to feel and be loved. The desire to be seen and heard entwines with this unseen energy that is like a magnet that pulls us toward our inner self and others.

We all have a love language that speaks to the heart. This can reflect in self-love and love for others. These love languages are Words of Affirmation, Physical Touch, Receiving Gifts, Quality Time, and Acts of Service. Each has attributes of communication, actions to take, and what to avoid. When we are living in our truths and authenticity and teaching others our love language, the world is a magical place to be.

In the rising mist of the morning dew
We embrace the new sun rising,
With eagerness and anticipation
Of life's twisted, winding roads.

The unknown before us
Gives way to creation,
Of what we envision
Through the kaleidoscope of mystery.

The heart knows best of what has meaning
Letting go of strife and sorrow.
Keeping hope within the grasp of
Tight fists thrust upwards towards the sky.

As we fly with our wings of glory,
Triumphant and celebrating.
What we know is our truths,
That love conquers all.

As the evening dusk falls upon the land,
Bringing stillness to the night.
We look out at the starlight velvet blanket
Winking back at us with promise.

That tomorrow brings new opportunities
For peace and serenity.
Bow your head in prayer for what is yet to come,
An amazing sense of gratitude.

Ride the wings of the angels into the light,
Snuff out the darkness of yesteryear and
See the beauty of today.
Love is the answer, always ready to share......

Love is the greatest force in the universe that gives healing and life, binds souls together, and whispers in our ears that all will be well.

A mother's love is unconditional and can transcend time, space, and potential obstacles. The connection goes beyond words, for she knows the child better than they know themselves. She provides comfort, reassurance, and guidance all their lives. She becomes their guiding light, offering wisdom and instilling confidence and resilience.

In relationships, love is a dance between the masculine and the feminine, the yin and the yang, and the mind and the heart. Romantic love is a passion to experience life to the fullest, and there is a maturity that binds two people together. When two people meet, they are naïve and young in the development of the relationship, regardless of their age. Getting to know the other person takes time, understanding, listening, and non-judgment. Love eventually breaks through the cracks of the barriers of the past, walls built, and weakened inner spirit.

The seven-year itch represents the time when two people may begin to feel a pull away from their current partner. You may ask why this happens. It seems that the drive to continue to build on the relationship and purposefully focus on personal and spiritual development together somehow gets lost in the journey. Life happens.

The good news is, there is a way to not only survive this ominous period but also to thrive beyond it. Love is always present; you can close your eyes and take yourself inward. With a steady breath, feel the outer world fade, and it is just you and the expansive universal space. Allow yourself to bring forth the connection to a source bigger than the self. In this oneness, all that is, a sense of freedom will be felt. By infusing the energy and how you feel in this moment, you enable the expansion of love to become a part of you, to be you.

When we are weathered by life, holding onto the pains, hurts, injustice, judgments, and unfairness, we deny ourselves and others the opportunities to be the authentic selves we were born as. Love is an asset for us to honor and respect, as it overrides all other feelings and emotions. It is the driving force that can determine our ability to experience the beauty of life itself.

By releasing attachments and thoughts of how another person *should* be, the tethers that bind us together beautifully transform everything about us and the world around us. The heart center strengthens bringing new experiences, perspectives, and paths upon which we can choose to walk. Love comes in many shapes and sizes, none of which is right or wrong.

Love is not something we find; it winds its way into us by circumstances and our responses. A declaration of what we want can catapult us into an incredible ocean of ebb and flow, the magnetic pull of what is unseen, serendipitously blending two souls. There is an undeniable attraction, sometimes in a push-pull way, as the dance of union evolves into a settling of the heart and spirit.

I won't give up on us,
No matter how rough the seas.

I give you all my love,

Giving you the space to navigate.

Who I am is within the world we create,
You have come so far.

Take my hand and sail with me into
the winds of time and space.

There is no bond stronger,
Than Love.

Together we unite and
Change the world....

The growth and development of a person signifies letting go of expectations and giving room for the individual journey within the union of the whole. Appreciation is the magic infused within the words spoken and actions taken. By appreciating everything the other person brings into any relationship, you solidify the basis of the relationship and the love that grows and blossoms. Love will grow stronger, amplifying trust, compassion, courage, and confidence. There is no need for anything other than walking each moment side-by-side, holding hands, and witnessing the beauty of life's most precious gift. That, which *is* love.

~Eileen Bild

Introduction

What is love? This one question precedes all the mysteries of the universe. It bounces around in my head like a pinball, a never-ending query in a loop of uncertainty as to where it will finally stop. Not only that question, but also, many other questions bubble up to the surface … my mind chuckles in resonance with itself. Oh, so many questions … when will they stop? My intrigued heart says, "Go deep, and even deeper." My mind says, "No, I can't!" Then I hear a tiny whisper come up from the mysterious depths; it says with a smirk, "You have to; you're writing a book about love!" I inquire, "But … why is love so hard and difficult to figure out? Maybe it's just me, and I'm making it much harder than it is. Is it really that simple?" I settle down and dive in.

Welcome, dear reader, to *Mission Hope, Volume III*, in the series; a book with 20 brilliant writers/authors who accepted the challenge in a courageous attempt to answer this and many other questions from their real-life experiences on the subject of love. It seems to be the most difficult one to write of all three of the Mission Hope books to date.

We are writing to help the world find hope, faith, grace, joy, and gratitude through love. But is that even possible? We believe it is. The enlightening stories to follow are valuable and varied but all true. Through love, we have overcome so much of what life has thrown at us. I believe love healed me of breast cancer 4x! "But how?" you might ask. It was more than hope and faith; I had a lot of that too.

I know that some of you may be having a bit of difficulty with the subject of love. And, honestly, I was too. I have been thinking and meditating on it consistently, asking for quick answers. One morning, in meditation, I had an out-of-body experience—an epiphany, if you will. The following is what came to me. See if any of this resonates with you. Let's talk about it.

Does love only show up in fairy tales; romance novels; or in passionate, steamy personal encounters? Is love worth dying for? Or is it for learning to find the incredible beauty of life through it? Or both? And how has love shown up for you? Are you still searching aimlessly for it? Is love external to oneself? Or do you keep it self-contained? Has love changed or healed you in some way? How? How has love been a healing factor or force in your life?

In really going deep into love, we realize it is not often truly shown by the giver or received by the receiver. Why do you think not? Love is not superficial; it is given and received by and through the HEART. Love pierces the hardest of souls and softens them. Do you believe you are worthy of love? Is love an entitlement? If love is free, why do some go to extremes to feel they must somehow pay for love? Love is not just a fleeting moment. Love is not earned or sacrificed. Is love even definable? Is love really more than just a feeling? How does it feel to you?

I have to admit this is a tough subject for me to talk about. How about you? Some shy away from giving and accepting love. Is it hard or easy for you to say "I love you"? Do you feel more comfortable just saying "Love you" instead? Why? Is love gender-specific? Were you raised by people who told you they loved you or not? Or did you feel it was conditional love? What is unconditional love anyway?

These are all very deep and personal questions. Love is a deep emotion. We believe answering them, or attempting to, will help heal our world ... and ourselves. It starts with me and you; it starts with us! Let's dive in and dive in deep. Nothing superficial will make a difference. We are the difference-makers, the change-makers, the way-showers. I understand the subject is deeply personal. Some have shied away from talking about it because maybe it hurts too much. And that's OK. You who are here are the chosen ones. Yes, you're here for a reason. A very important one.

It's OK to still not know all the answers or even have a clue. Most of us honestly are still on the journey of learning what love really means. Standing on the precipice of love, I ask you, is there more than one definition? Of course, love is multifaceted. Like the beautiful diamond that represents it.

I'm not sure anyone can ever truly answer all or any of these deeply personal questions. Some are still searching for the answer to just one of them. How can love be enough to save someone's life? Think about that. That is the power of love!

What would you add to this list of questions? Do you have any of the answers? I think the answers will vary from person to person due to family and cultural conditioning and learning. We, the authors of this book, want to know what you, our readers, think. We hope that our stories here will shed some valuable light on the subject.

Take our hands as we, together, delve into the platinum vault of the heart of love and attempt to answer some of your inquiries with these inspiring stories. Ready, let›s go!

Enjoy!

With indelible love,
Char Murphy

Fearless Love

—

Karen Ortega

The previous two books of Mission Hope were just the beginning of my unfolding story about hope, faith, and the wounding abuse that bared down on me daily. One day recently, there was a substantial change in the wind, unbeknownst to me. This third chapter in my ever-evolving story, for *Volume III*, brought new exposure to something much deeper and something I was unaware of that was the actual reason for my lifetime of heartache and struggles. Generational abuse and the lack of unconditional love. The signs were all there pointing to my childhood and forgiving my family, but it took me a while to see and accept it. I thought my family was relatively normal and that sharp tongues and emotional attacks were just part of the family dynamics of most. It's glaringly obvious now, of course, but I don't think I was ready to see it then. God knows better than I do, and at the right time, I was shown what I needed to heal. Unfortunately, the information was not well received by my family. I was blacklisted and an outcast for writing about it in these books. They are not ready to see, which means I let go and move on. I was silenced for so long that I refuse to be silenced anymore. I refused to be engaged in this angry, abusive energy any longer, and that includes my part in it because of what I was taught and experienced.

I was born with a deeply sensitive and emotional Scorpio energy, and my kind-hearted self struggled hard to accept the lot I was given. Family is family, and you have to love them, no matter what they are doing, right?

No. You can love from a distance and forgive them from afar. I almost couldn't stand myself because I was told how bad I was my whole life. I had sad anger at a young age as far back as I can remember. I believe now that the sadness came in the tones of this generational abuse imparted to me at birth and the consistency with which I was critiqued, judged, and abused growing up—even into adulthood. It never let up. Even at work, I would encounter much hate directed at me. I didn't even have to speak to have it show up. It further battered my self-esteem, and coworkers were baffled by me being singled out. I laugh about it now because I know why. I didn't love myself, and it was showing up everywhere to show me. But I also had coworkers cheering me on and encouraging me to step into something bigger. It's funny because one of the old bosses who was so mean at one time showed up at my workplace from 900 miles away, and the moment she saw me, she ran up and hugged me and asked how I was doing. I felt her forgiveness in that one moment. It was beautiful!

The many experiences in life made me stronger and wiser, and I'm using them for strength and wisdom on my way as I walk my own path. It was showing me which way to swim instead of treading water, and it's no longer suffering and punishment that my overthinking mind so easily doled out to me. It's how I chose to look at it, and it was a hard lesson to learn, but in the end, it was my fearless soul and fearless love that pushed me onward.

There was, at that time and space, no acceptance of myself or my emotions, and the push and pull within myself left me heartbroken and totally misunderstood by others and confused myself. I went through a bitter and resentful stage, but it was just a passing-through stage to love. It was like walking over a bridge with resentment on one side and love on the other, and I was stuck somewhere in between. I hated myself for a time, and it was not what I wanted but was simply the process I needed to go through to move to the other side and into love and acceptance not only of myself but of others. I may get some backlash for this hate space, but understand that it was just what I needed to protect myself and move into a place where I could love myself. I won't go over the details of this as I outlined it in the first and second Mission Hope books previously. It was such a process for me, and no one could ever understand it but me. It took me a while, but I eventually came to understand that my family's generational abuse is what had me hooked in. I honestly did not know how to untangle myself from it.

I still love my family, no matter how they see me, and I just didn't know for a long time that it was due to emotional abuse within my family lineage. The women were exceptionally hard and judgmental of each other and sadly missing compassion and understanding. They still do not understand this. The critical and judgmental life I experienced was cruel and unjust at times. I never felt like I fit in, and trying to love them and accept their behavior (backstabbing and betrayal) left a chasm that I couldn't bridge. As a child, it left me with emotional baggage that now, in adulthood, was fodder for my family, which further deepened the childhood wound of rejection, and that in turn caused me to reject myself as an adult. It was in this undoing of myself, this rejection, that the bandages started to fall away. I was left with nothing but myself because I sometimes pushed people away like my family did to one another. I started to understand that I, in fact, was missing my own love and self-acceptance. I never fathomed the idea of just "letting them be" who they are and saying what they want without being hurt by it. It takes a graceful strength to walk away from sharp tongues and not take it personally. It hurt my sensitive soul; I won't lie. I had to form the part of me that didn't care what they said about me. I had to shift the power back to me because they knew I was an easy target to hurt. I refuse now to let that happen anymore.

Self-acceptance and learning to love yourself for all that you are has been and will be the greatest lesson about love for you, regardless of how others see you or how you were taught to see yourself. It was for me. I've learned some emotional maturity along the way and how to keep my crown on and keep on stepping. As a child and now an adult, I just wanted to love and be loved and accepted for being me all along. It was a dance that had to be balanced. What anyone else sees me as is none of my business. I will always love my family, but walking away is what I did for my own well-being and to break the chain of abuse and rejection. I hope one day they will read this and understand.

Something else that was a pivotal moment was, with generational abuse comes generational poverty. If you don't love yourself (low self-worth), it sets you on the road of poverty and "lack thinking," and this was a big one for me. Huge aha moment of awareness! If you hold onto resentments and don't forgive, then money is not magnetized to you. So, remember, love equals prosperity. It's a bit of a tricky road for me. The deep scars needed to be healed to let love in. Forgiveness, I have learned, is easier for some than it was for me. One of my most beautiful moments and one where the weight fell off was after asking God why life is such a struggle, what was the block to abundance for me, and my way out of poverty. Loving myself was the answer that came—and forgiving those who hurt me, no matter what they did or didn't do. That is love's highest calling, and this is where life had been leading me. All of the lack resulted from the resentments and unforgiveness from the past. All of the broken relationships came from not loving myself and choosing people that reflected that, but they were also there as teachers. Hard-won lesson, but damn am I grateful to be given the opportunity to understand. Generational abuse had me stuck in a really critical cycle within myself. It keeps everyone embroiled and really combative. It is also where low-self-esteem breeds. This is hard to write, but it's the truth, and it's important to say.

We are here to enjoy life and be happy, but we have to love ourselves first for that abundance to show up. We have to let go of the resentments. It's the only way. This is so huge and so appropriate right now. It's your way out of poverty and lack. Remember this one key fact; it will set you free. Love equals prosperity. We think into existence what we are. Low self-esteem brings lack. Once I understood this, there was the sweeping realization of why my lack and that of my family's struggles with it. Boom! Now I'm ready for a change! No way do I want life to be a struggle. I would be willing to forgive myself and others for life to be joyful! But hold on! I wish it was that easy to just drop it. For me, it wasn't; for you, maybe so … it's a process as I write this.

For the time being, I had to let go of my family so I could understand what was missing in myself and learn to love me. I couldn't do it with the past and the same people who are still in that space. Understand that they are only operating in what they know, and I am hopeful one day, they, too, will pull out of it. I am still pulling out of it myself. I pray every day to help change the conditioning inside of me. I am still a deep-feeling, truly loving, and caring soul, and that will never change. I love myself for that one single thing.

Hold onto your hats as the wind begins to blow, as sometimes it does. Some other things I learned; it was no longer about who hurt me, who left the deepest scars, or that I was labeled "too emotional" or "too sensitive." It wasn't about the rage I sometimes felt or how much I cried sometimes or even feeling like a misfit in my own family. My journey was a spiritual one that they would never understand or accept. I understand now, and forgiveness is all that is left for me to do. Forgiving myself was priority number one. I brought to myself these experiences for my own evolution. I understand that it was part of my lesson of self-love, self-acceptance, and self-compassion, and as hard as it was to not react to some of my family's behaviors toward me, I had to take responsibility for myself and not judge them for it. Change doesn't take place on the turning wheel; it comes from stepping off and changing the way I do things. That's where it stops; this is where the cycle ends. The moment I disengaged from the combativeness I learned from this generational abuse was the moment I won, and love took hold. The ceasing of the tongues brings a silence that speaks volumes. I am the curse breaker of this generational abuse in my family. I know my ancestors are helping, and I hope I can help anyone else who has been impacted by the turmoil of generational abuse in its different forms.

I am gathering up my energy, knowing I am doing my very best on the backs of my ancestors who came before me, who couldn't break the stronghold, and I do not care what anyone thinks of me anymore. I am stepping up to bring awareness to this subject. I am a humble, simple me who loves animals, collecting rocks, bird nests, and pressing flowers. I am a tree lover and have a child-like curiosity and enthusiasm, and I love protecting the earth the best way I can in my little "neck of the woods." I am loving and understanding; I am compassionate; I am empathic and very sensitive; and I have the right to be all these things, including sometimes angry.

Generational abuse has had its hand in my upbringing; in the ways I love, in which I operate; how I feel; and in my overall well-being, and I am strong enough to realize it, understand it, and break its chains. I am strong enough to talk about it without guilt, shame, or fear because there is no other way to break the hold it has until I can see it in a new light. I AM that light.

When I wasn't shown respect, I didn't know how to ask for it or how to teach people to show it to me. I didn't know relationships should be mutually respectful. Often life showed me the opposite. Abusive relationships are where I drifted until now because my eyes and heart are open to what is in front of me—all the lessons and the pain. It was all on my learning and growth path, just passing through; it was never going to stay. I only had to start looking up instead of down for it to pass. This is part of my love lesson. It is part of my coming of age, if you will, of me becoming the better version of myself and bringing into awareness that which isn't unconditional love.

Generational abuse was hard on my soul; it ripped me apart from the inside. It made me drift for a while, in and out of who I was, who I wasn't, and who I thought I should be. The brain fog, depression, and deep need for unconditional love and respect; love wasn't lost on me. Let people do what they do and watch without reaction and then determine if they stay or go. I waited and even begged for apologies, clarity, and understanding that never came. Then I asked myself, "Do I really need an apology from the very people who knew they were hurting me?" Maybe I wanted it, but do I really need it? Do I have to have that to heal my heart? The answer is NO. Forgive and move on. Can it really be that easy? Probably not, as the pain is deeply ingrained.

Generational abuse isn't always the critical, judgmental, and unforgiving type. In my experience, I have seen it also look like love but be masked with manipulation and jealousy. The biggest and most egregious is the emotional harm that comes on its heels and the poverty mindset that is generated because of the lack of love and compassion for one another. Hate, bitterness, and anger can't generate anything that is love; just poverty in all things. Forgiveness and love are the catalysts to abundance and a good life. Forget possessions; let's think of joy, peace, and love instead for yourself and everyone you know. That's abundance.

We have to make peace with ourselves and others. Love attracts, and hate dissipates. It's taking me a long time to understand this. Loving ourselves is key to abundance. If we love ourselves, we have way more compassion and empathy for those fighting their own battles.

I used the anger to help me change. It was really the catalyst that propelled me out. I used this same upheaval for self-acceptance and standing up for myself. Self-acceptance for everything I was taught to be so I could change it and then instill it with love. I had this triggering anger from the many years of abuse, and I had to overcome it. The same people who triggered me were reminding me of my childhood of abuse I needed to forgive.

Looking back at the experience, it was very empowering in terms of what I gained from it—independence, confidence, self-investment, personal power, and the power of choice. The experience and life lessons are in my belt, and I've learned how to move mentally from this place. I look at this from a perspective of love and the experiences as hard lessons that were needed for my own leveling up. I now understand why a little better.

Talking about it helps me let go, and I feel more love and more understanding of my life in general and that of my family. I ask for divine assistance daily to alleviate my mind and soul and to heal me from any turmoil that floats in, and sometimes it still does, but I am definitely healing from it. I know this because I no longer wake up to my mind going to war, as it always took my body with it. That is no longer happening—and it is such a blessing to wake up, feeling peace in my mind. It's also very important to ask for healing for others, too, as they walk their own life path.

Because of the years of abuse, it is a steady but slow process of healing, and I'm grateful for this because patience is needed for change. Letting go of the old self and the ways you were brought up takes a steady and loving hand, and that is where I am as I write this. It's a call now for me to talk about generational abuse, the deep shame, guilt, and being the curse breaker and the outcast for speaking up. There is nothing to be ashamed of. It is simply something passed down; recognizing that and changing the perspective of how you see it and making a change from there takes a fearless soul and a fearless kind of love. This is how love appeared to me: it was in the darkness that it showed itself, and once the light of love shone upon it, I was able to see what I was missing and what had returned to me. There is no greater joy or love than that!

It takes a village of strong-leveled-up people to help a sister who is struggling to get there. All of the strong beautiful souls of Mission Hope were so kind and loving and helped me see through my limited perception from the bruises of life. It was here that I started to understand that this is a new level of love and what unconditional love is all about. This is what family should look and feel like, and it was what was missing in childhood that stunted me in adulthood. Now I see, eyes wide open, the quest to know myself, with the help of those who are inspiring beings of light around me, the Mission Hope co-authors, and my beautiful friend Char Murphy, the creator of the books; they all helped me gain strength, grace, and an even deeper level of compassion. I am so thankful to be a part of this family and book series. May these books light up the world! May each story touch a soul and propel them forward.

I call on everyone to rise up. We need you now to lift the light of this world. I call on everyone who has suffered and all those who are lights in the world already. May the helper people come to assist. We need your hurt—your brokenness—to step forward, but we also need your faith, love, and conviction to bring yourself to the edge and be fearless in all you do!

I want to leave you with a tiny piece that helped me let go of resentments. I said it every time a harsh thought floated in until it withered away. "I release unto God: I wish for (name) all of God's peace, joy, and happiness."

Love, love, love ... to all of you reading this!

About Karen Ortega

 Karen D. Ortega is a best-selling author, and this is her third book in the Mission Hope series. She is a free-spirited soul who grew up with a humble and adventurous life on a farm near St. Louis, Missouri, with her family. She moved to NW Florida in 2012 and is enjoying life and the comfort of the warm, sunny days near the Gulf Coast. She is a mother to three adult children and 13 grandchildren, including one great-grandchild. She loves animals and has six dogs and one cat and would have more if she could. She loves road trips, writing, drawing and painting, homecooked meals, and spending time with those she loves. Her adventurous spirit and wandering soul are something she uses to enjoy all the moments in her life that come her way. She lives each day with hope and believes in the power of yourself to bring dreams alive and live your best life. Joy and happiness are above all her biggest themes for herself and all who know her. Karen's dream is to buy a 300-acre farm and farmhouse for her forever home where she can have an animal sanctuary and a staging place for magical gatherings for all those who wish for a change in the wind.

Love Language of Presence

Brad Burchnell

Have you ever been in a moment feeling that "perfect love," and it wasn't anything grand or elaborate? It was a place of pure contentment, looking at that moment with no expectations but knowing that you are love for someone else. That perfect moment is not a feeling; it is a choice. You are choosing to be fully present with someone else and casting any distractions far from you so that you can be there fully.

I have seen the opposite for many years. I know that this was the case for me. I would be thinking about what to say next, but I wasn't present. I would be thinking of how to show someone how right I was; I wasn't present. I would engage in discussions online, be on my cellphone, or do exercises or anything else rather than be present for those that I loved. I rationalized my actions by working hard and placing value on money, accolades, recognition, and acceptance from others, external, external, external, and I omitted the important over the temporary.

How many of us do that each day and erode that loving relationship that was so important at the beginning but is now a competition of who's right, who has had the worst day, who has contributed more in the household, or who is contributing to the welfare of the family? It boils down to not being intentional and not choosing presence, otherwise known as quality time.

We are not present, and we are less, and we are minimizing the most important people in our lives, not providing the gift of quality time, otherwise known as presence. When we fail in this precious area, we reduce the importance of connection and being there at the most important times for those we love. In the end, it is not what we could accumulate; it is rather the time that we wish we could have back. It is gone. I want you to experience the greatest love through gaining a greater understanding of presence.

A Picture is Worth a Thousand Words

While I was recovering from the loss of my daughter and the loss of my marriage, I decided to go out one day. Though my world had crumbled, I put on a "painted face" of someone happy as I entered the restaurant. I mindlessly engaged in conversation with my server. I then began to wait for my meal as I sipped on my coffee and watched the patrons all around me. I was surrounded by people—couples not talking, moms with their kids unengaged (all of them looking at their electronic screens)—and felt a chill within. It was in those very moments that the enormity of my previous actions and behaviors sank in, and I took full responsibility for my past. It was a lot knowing all of the choices that I had made, and worse yet, knowing that I had chosen poorly. Have you been there?

The starkest illustration that I can share is when I saw this one particular couple around my age sitting near my table, and they were eating in complete silence. They weren't looking at their phones (not that I saw any with them); they weren't talking and were not even looking at one another. They sat in a silence that I could classify as, "enormously loud." After they completed their meal, they got up and departed without one word being spoken, except to their server. When had talking with one another become such a burden? Why had we lost the ability to choose love and connection? It was right then that I felt a profound wave of emotion and sadness wash over me. It was at that moment that I gained profound clarity, resulting in a near-audible decision: whatever might happen in the future, I was going to be present for others and myself.

So, let me ask this question of you, dear reader: how does this picture resonate with you? Is it a picture of where you currently are in your relationships? Does it bother you greatly? Does it not bother you at all? Or do you wish to read more of the changes that can be made to have a deeper love connection not only with others but within yourself as well? It takes a great amount of courage to be vulnerable with yourself, enough to admit and accept that there are changes that are required to be made.

Each day, I see disconnectedness, people with their noses directly against a screen, all the while with someone wanting their attention. The wife who is feeling alone and isolated; the vulnerable husband reaching out to others because of the disconnectedness that he feels within his relationship with his spouse; the kids feeling overwhelmed by life through cyberbullying and not feeling that they are seen or heard by their parents due to their disconnectedness with them; and the list goes on.

So, this is a really encouraging start, isn't it? By all accounts, most people (including me) would have checked out and thrown in the towel. I want to encourage you to continue reading, as love does make a difference, and that first love is you. It allows you to love others with abundance and attention. You give of yourself through your presence because you value it above all else. It doesn't mean sacrificing everything; it does mean a vital shift in your approach and perspectives to living, loving, and being.

Learning and Learned Moments

It's most difficult for us to admit when we fall short because we desire to be right in all cases, and often that is what separates us from others. Our steadfast thought is that we are the center of the universe and all things in the world. Let me give you an example; I was out to dinner, and my youngest daughter was with me. I was busy on my cellphone and clickety-clicketing away. The next thing I knew, my youngest had taken my cellphone and told me, "Dad, I want to see your face and talk. I can't do that with you scrolling and typing through dinner." I was not happy for several reasons. Today, I can say it is an embarrassment. Here I was, a grown adult who really loved spending time with his family. I worked hard and long to get the "things" that I thought would make me happy and them as well.

My daughter wanted my presence, and I was slow to understand this valuable lesson. When I responded angrily, her demeanor totally changed. Today, it is a moment that I deeply regret and one that I can never get back. That was a learning moment, the turning point, and today, it is a learned moment that I apply each day. Fast forward many years while out with my fiancée and her granddaughters. They are typical in some ways and not in others. We all went out shopping for them prior to the school year. They are very different, but both are deeply independent with great style. I had my phone put away, as I gave it to my fiancée to put in her purse. I wanted to give them the gift of my presence.

We had the opportunity to spend the entire day together. We went through so many different stores, and I even saw some really nice outfits for them to try on. They are constantly amazed at how I (a male) can see fashions that would look good on them. They always say (with a smile), "We forget sometimes that you are the dad of girls." I modeled putting my phone away and asked them to do the same as we were out. They asked me why. I told them that their grandmother and I wanted a gift from both of them. They looked at us, puzzled, and finally said, "How much do you want us to spend?" I looked at them both and told them this, "It is a kind of expense, some might say, but we want the gift of your full attention and presence this afternoon, with your phones off, unless your mom and dad call or text you. Can you do that for us?" We got home later after dark and went to the backyard where their parents were sitting by the firepit. They excitedly told them all about their day. Their dad asked, "Did you have a good day, and did you say thank you?" I assured their mom and dad that they are the most wonderful girls and are always appreciative of what we do with thank-yous. Before they went upstairs to prepare for bed, more hugs, thank-yous, and I-love-yous were shared.

The gift of presence is never undervalued. It is only undervalued by those of us who fail to heed the lessons that are offered to us to learn. We can grow from these examples and illustrations, in that paying attention to the little things weaves a greater opportunity to love deeply and richly. Shared experiences in the things that are important to others and paying attention to the things that are important to them is a lesson that has not been lost upon me.

CBMs (AKA: Character Building Moments)

My dad, when he was alive, loved illustrations; most called them CBs, and my brother and I began to loathe the term. To this day, it is not one of my favorite things to accept, but it is one that I lean into for greater understanding. We spend so much time on negative energy that we fail to embrace the special moments by embracing the lessons learned to become the person that we deserve to become.

I had just gotten my driver's license, and I was not a good driver at all. I hit another car from behind. My dad arrived and took control as I fell apart. I remember nothing about that day, except being absolutely petrified of what would happen. *How much trouble would I be in? How loud would my dad yell at me?* Instead, he hugged me and told me he loved me and was grateful that everyone was OK. He then told me on the way home, "That was a hard CB, wasn't it?" I nodded yes, with tears running down my face.

Growing up is so difficult but indeed built upon CBs that enable our understanding of the world through active learning. Through it all, it is also built upon love, though we might not fully comprehend it at the time we are experiencing it. I was learning another component of love through my dad's presence in a moment of inconvenience. How he responded; rather than with anger, he showed me love through his compassion and kind understanding.

Fast forward many years past, I received a message that one of my daughters had been involved in an accident that totaled her car; airbags deployed, and all the things going with it. I sent a quick message to my boss that I was heading out because my daughter was in an accident. As I was driving home, many thoughts kept running through my mind. I was in total flashback mode to my first accident and thought, *How am I going to show up today?* When I arrived, she was crying, and all I wanted to do was hug her and tell her how much I loved her. She kept saying "I killed my car" and that she was sorry, as I had just purchased it for her. I told her, "Don't worry; cars can be replaced; you can't." Then I shared my experience with my first car accident and her grandfather's words to me. It was a CB moment revisited for me. I was present!

Love, Marriage, Everything In-Between, and What It All Means

While I began to write this whole chapter, I wanted to get a perspective of what love means. Is it spiritual, humanistic, sacrificial, biblical, or somewhere in between? Words and intents matter a great deal; at least they do to me. Anyone else? So, what is love? What does it mean? How does it relate to being present?

I found some truly treasured ones on a website called RatioChristi:

Hessed – Lovingkindness

Dod – Romantic love

Eros – Sexual love

Phileo – Fraternal love

Agape – Sacrificial love

Storge – Familial love

These had aspects of what I knew and had experienced about love, but I still hadn't found the true meaning of presence and love. *Was love situational? Was it merely a feeling? Was it deeper than that? What is love?*

I began to seek deeper within and seek wisdom as I began to unravel my own value system and pillars of my core values to live a life free of my past. Then I found a brilliant nugget in this, "Your presence is required." This phrase is often found on invitations. It means they need you to show up and be there as a witness, as someone who is valued, as someone who is dearly loved.

This is exactly how we should view ourselves to show up for ourselves without respect to anything external. It is, at the very core, a decision that we make daily. It is not something that should fade with our feelings. I will say that I did not practice this in the past, and if we are honest, I am not sure many of us could or did. It is something that I have incorporated into who I am and is not just a trivial thing that can be turned on or off. Intentional action, knowing that you love yourself first, allows you to be fully present in all situations, regardless of any "feeling." Feelings come and go, but the daily decisions made to be present for yourself and for others is love.

It is not easy, and it never was meant to be. That is something that I am learning each day. I told my fiancée the reasons and how I fell in love with her, and each day, I fall in love with her more and want to be present at all times, whether in the good times or the difficult ones. I make the decision each day to love her and to consistently be present, not because of a feeling or an obligation. It is given freely, and though it is a season of her experiencing another round of cancer, it is also one of abiding love to be present with her. She helps me to desire and strive to be a better man; she shows up for me each day. She is present.

Coming full circle, we are present in all things and all ways. Each of us, each day, chooses. Will you choose to be present? Will you choose love? Presence is quality time, and quality time is love. Choosing presence is choosing love through our presence. I've chosen presence and love.

About Brad Burchnell

 Brad Burchnell is the founder of From My Heart to Yours, LLC, located in Roseville, MI, providing grief support and coaching, along with suicide prevention advocacy, as well as speaking offerings to businesses, educational institutions, and non-profits. His direct experiences with the loss of his daughter to suicide in 2018 and his father to cancer in 1980, along with leading and assisting with the facilitation of grief support groups for over seven years, provide him with a unique perspective. Brad has a diverse background of writing, collaborative efforts, and being featured in such works as:

- *Journey Well; You Are More Than Enough* by Mariah and Byron Edington
- *Scars to Stars – Volume 2,* (contributing author) an anthology, by Deanna Mitchell
- *Lightbulb Moments: Through the Eyes of Men – Terrifying, Traumatic, Triumphant - Stories of Hope,* a collection by Kerrie Atherton
- *From My Heart To Yours – I am Not My Mistakes* by Brad Burchnell
- *Mission Hope: Thriving Through Seasons of the Soul* – Co-author
- *Mission Hope: Inspirational Stories of Faith and Hope* – Co-author
- Numerous podcasts and live-streaming events

He has served in leadership that includes serving in the US Navy as a Chief Petty Officer in the field of Meteorology and Oceanography for 15 years and senior positions in manufacturing that included serving as the onsite senior executive. He served as a leader and assistant leader facilitating faith-based grief support for over seven years. He is a graduate of Fresno State University, where he received his bachelor's degree in Industrial Technology and Manufacturing, as well as post-graduate work in the field of counseling from Trinity College of the Bible and Theological Seminary. He is blessed with an amazing fiancée, a large extended family, a son-in-law married to his oldest surviving daughter and grandson, and his youngest daughter is seeking a master's degree at Grand Rapids Theological Seminary.

The Secret Ingredient

—

Meche Barba

Since times that memory can't be recounted, families have gathered around food. As time evolved, culinary art was developed and passed on from generation to generation, creating recipes that became the signature element of celebrating different occasions. Some of them involved rituals and practice, requiring days of preparation ahead of a certain event. Some other ones, more on the comfort food side, were easy but undeniably delicious, always leaving an imprint on the memory of those who were eating them.

Our lineage, even though complicated and with a plethora of karmic challenges, was always blessed with extraordinary cooking abilities. Each one of the members of our family was and still is full of creativity; we are problem solvers and analytical thinkers with a huge heart filled with joy and care for our families.

When I turned one year old, back then, it was always a special event to be celebrated with friends and family. My grandma, together with my mom, planned the event. Then, with her maid, she went to the kitchen and prepared all kinds of delicacies for the people invited to the celebration. My mother recalls her preparing small meringues that she would put together in pairs and fill with whipped cream. She was a very strong woman, despite being short and slim. She despised the advancements of modernity and all those new gadgets suddenly joining her sacred space, the kitchen. Instead of joining the wave, she would do it all by hand. She would beat dozens of egg whites by hand; she would prepare the most amazing puff pastry in huge batches and fold and turn them in a whiff. The table was filled with all kinds of hors d'oeuvres, savory dishes, and marvelous desserts.

Her cooking was famous and loved by all throughout the city. Friends and family, even though some of them were unattended, would pass by to visit my grandparents right before lunchtime so that they could stay and join them at the table. She was an extremely generous woman, and she would never deny a plate of food to anyone. The table at my grandparent's house was huge. More than 20 people could easily be seated around it. Meals were always a time of love, joy, and celebration. Grandma's very special way of showing love was through her cooking.

My mother comes from Medellin in Colombia, a city where the weather is hot, and meals are completely different from the ones in our beautiful Quito located in the Andean region of Ecuador, at a high altitude, and back then, with rainy, cold weather most of the time. When my parents moved from Medellin to Quito, my mom felt out of place in many senses, and food was no exception to the rule. She wouldn't even risk trying most of grandma's dishes, surviving mostly on eggs, bread, and coffee. Knowing that the situation was becoming sort of desperate, my grandma suggested my mom go to the kitchen and ask the maid to prepare her the food she liked. My mother found refuge in her solitude and feeling homesick, joining her at the kitchen table, sharing stories about both families, and finally getting some food that resembled what she used to eat in her native Medellin.

The maid would go to the public market every single day to buy fresh ingredients to prepare food for the family. There, she found the so-called *caldo de gallina*, a chicken soup with potatoes they added chopped green onions and coriander to, and took a portion to my mom.

My mom told me years after that looking back at those times, she felt as if she was behaving like a spoiled rotten brat, but my grandma with her patience and care won her heart through food. Bit by bit, she started trying her mother-in-law's delicious recipes, and then she realized what she had been missing all those months of her refusing to eat that wonderful food.

At some point in 1965, my mother had a miscarriage, which left a deep mark in her heart. Not being able to get pregnant was a source of frustration. There were some periods when she would stay in bed all day and also when she was sick in bed. On one of those occasions, my grandma baked her famous "bizcochitos," some salted cookies prepared with cream, that literally melt in your mouth. My grandparents lived in a huge mansion with several floors, and my parents were living in an apartment on the second floor. They would join the family for the main meals every day. Going back to the salted cookies, my grandma brought my mom a huge tin jar filled with them for her to eat while in bed. She left it, and when she came back, she noticed her daughter-in-law had almost finished them. She refilled the tin jar with the cookies to the top again.

Some people desperately need to hear the words "I love you," but the other person can't express that, and they can feel frustrated and angry because of that. In my mother's case, she understood that all those little details went beyond what words can tell. It was my grandma's way of showing her love and care toward her daughter-in-law.

I was not yet four years old when my grandma passed away, but before that, remarkably, I vividly remember visiting her at her house, and she was always happy to see me. I remember one time when we were both sitting at the dining room table, and she was peeling some mandarin oranges for me. She would carefully open each one of the wedges and take all the seeds out before giving them to me. Those fond memories have stayed with me forever.

My grandma, my mother's mom, visited my parents when they were still living at my other grandma's place. Throughout the following years and all the way until her passing, she would usually stay in Quito for some months, and then she would go back to Colombia to visit my aunts. Our place was the one she considered home. She had a wonderful relationship with my dad, so her stay was always something welcomed as a family.

My mother's mom was widowed when my mom was about 10 months old. When my grandpa died, she was left with nothing but her children. With three girls to take care of, she had to return back to her parent's home in Medellin. She would help her mother do the chores in exchange for a place to stay and food for her kids. She was brought up surrounded by maids, and she didn't really know much about housekeeping, cooking, sewing, and such.

Some years later, she was able to get a house from the Saint-Vincent-de-Paul Society, where she could finally go live with her children as a family of their own. She learned how to cook, and she started to sell some meatloaf patties, which we call *albodigon*, basically a very savory and flavorful huge meatball that you would cook, slice, batter, and then fry individually. My aunt, as a young teenager, would wake up very early every day to deliver them to several corner stores where they were sold, and this became a source of income for the family.

Grandma was a very resourceful woman. She taught herself how to sew. The way she recounts it is that her first projects were a disaster, but after some trial and error, she started improving. Slowly but surely, she started creating beautiful dresses for her kids, and word spread so that some other women would go see her to sew their clothing. She became a seamstress, and that would also add to her income. My mom and her sisters were always well-dressed. Her motto was to have a clean, spotless place, and her kids impeccable, and that was her way of hiding her poverty and lack of resources.

When my mom married my dad, Grandma Julia came to live with us for the most part of the time. When she was at home, she would prepare some wonderful Colombian hearty meals, as well as some sweets and desserts.

Some afternoons, while watching TV, we would see her disappear into the kitchen. All of a sudden, that wonderful aroma of sugar and vanilla would start filling the house. We would hear her calling us to find her with *velitas* almost ready on the stove. *Velitas*, also known as *melcochas* in Ecuador, is a sort of candy made out of raw sugar and water you boil on the stove until it achieves soft ball syrup point, and it's ready to be poured on a tray covered with butter. I don't even remember how old I was, probably around six or seven years old, when she taught us how to work with it. Once it had cooled down a bit, she would give us our portion, and with our tiny little hands, we would start stretching it until it changed color from dark to caramel. Most of the time, we couldn't wait to finish the process, and we were already eating it from our own hands. She would take the biggest portion, stretch it, and then divide it into small, long pieces and would warn us it was for my mom. Nevertheless, we would always get a share from my mom's as well. What a delightful way she had of showing us how much she cared and loved us.

Many of the best and most memorable stories of our lives revolve around food. Gathering around a table and surrounded by friends and family left an undeniable mark on our hearts. Food is the secret ingredient that brings us together and shows us the love that sometimes people cannot express in words.

When my brother passed away, a chain of events was triggered. My parents' friends and our family, close and extended, showed their care, love, and support in many different ways. I remember clearly how some of my mom's friends came with food. There was something in the air that told them she had lost her will to live the minute she lost her child, so they came to the rescue to show us their support and how much they loved and cared for the whole family through food.

Some weeks later, my mom left for Colombia. She was trying to avoid reality; she felt the need to run away from her broken heart and her unbearable pain. Her sister and my grandma made sure to provide her with a nurturing place where she could stay for some weeks. My brother and I stayed with my dad, and even though he didn't know how to cook, he would cook rice and eggs. He would prepare our lunches; he would wash our clothes and iron them. I laugh about the fact that he was even ironing our school uniform socks, and he never did burn anything. How he did it, I have no clue.

Our neighbor, a beautiful angel disguised as a woman, was cooking our meals. Once we arrived home from school, she made sure to have our lunch ready. Her cooking was beyond words. So rich and flavorful that we were always delighted to eat it. Between the both of us, my brother was the one she loved the most. I remember vividly how she would come knocking at our door with a Pyrex of freshly baked desserts. One of them, which was my favorite, is the one that has stuck in my mind. There is a variety of very sweet ripe plantains called *maqueno* that she would slice in half and add raisins and meringue on top. She would keep it in the oven until the meringue was perfect, golden brown.

My grandma also used to prepare the most delicious chorizos we would ever try. The process was time-consuming. She would start by cleaning the casings, then blow them with air, and finally let them dry on top of the clothesline for some days before she could start the actual preparation. Once they were properly dried, she would start by chopping the meat and the bacon lard into very fine and small pieces before adding the spices and the salt. She would previously put the casings in water for them to soften before they could be filled with the mixture of meat, lard, and spices. She would take her time, and she would make sure no air bubbles were left inside, explaining that air would spoil the meat. She would then divide the long casing already filled with the mixture into individual chorizos about 15 cm long, tie them with a piece of rope, and hang them on the clothesline again, to be left to dry for several days. Once they were properly dried, they could be stored.

We couldn't wait until it was the right time for the chorizos to be ready. We were always counting the days, even the hours, to be able to enjoy such a wonderful treat. Once they were properly cured, grandma would cut individual ones and slice them lengthwise in the middle; she would fry them in a frying pan while she already had some corn arepas ready. Once they were out of the pan, she served them on a plate together with lemon wedges and an arepa for us to enjoy.

Her *sancocho*, a soup prepared with beef ribs, yucca chunks, potatoes, green and ripe plantains, was unbeatable. After my grandma passed away, one of the things my mother used to say was that she would never have a *sancocho* that tasted as good as the one her mom used to prepare in her life again.

Bistec, the Spanish version of beef steak, was another one of her signature dishes. Steaks of meat and potatoes in a base of lots of onions, garlic, peppers, and tomatoes, together with some spices, served with rice was a real treat as well.

Every Christmas, mom would prepare *natilla*, a dessert with milk, raw sugar, cinnamon, and cornstarch. That was one of the staple foods we would eat for as long as it lasted, together with *buñuelos*, some round fried balls prepared with tons of cheese, and *hojuelas*—a kind of fried cookie that we would take alone or with some sugar syrup on top. Oh what a life! The kitchen was a high-traffic area back in those days. We would come and go, stealing the hot *buñuelos* and *hojuelas*, freshly fried and just out of the frying pan, together with a wedge of *natilla* while my mother was preparing the rest of the meal for Christmas Eve.

Before my mother got married, it was my grandma who was taking care of preparing the food at home. She went on to take some cooking classes, but cooking was not her thing, as a matter of speaking.

My friend told me once that the creativity in the kitchen, sewing, embroidering, and all those apparently innate abilities are passed down from your ancestors, and you have to connect to the Universe to bring that knowledge back to the present moment. That's what I chose to believe, and I feel blessed and inspired by it every single time that I decide to prepare something for my family.

After having worked in an office for more than 10 years before meeting my father, my mom became a housewife and a stay-at-home mother. Her passion for cooking kicked in, and also thanks to the interest she showed in learning my grandma's recipes; she was able to gather quite a few that she would later prepare at home after grandma's passing.

Our beautiful Maquena, who was my father's nanny in the beginning, also gave my mom some of the recipes that my grandma used to prepare. My mom's cooking was a mixture of all those recipes with a mixture of European influence, the rich and still highly underrated Ecuadorian cooking, together with her Colombian roots. She was an amazing cook. Everything she prepared was absolutely delicious.

When my oldest daughter was born, I completely lost my appetite. Now I know that I was going through a postpartum depression that was never diagnosed. I don't even know if it was a thing that we would even discuss with our doctor back then. Anyway, I remember my mom being so worried that she was trying to persuade me to eat some food by preparing the most delicious recipes she could think of. One of them was a recipe she had written down, most likely from a TV show, which was prepared with chicken in a sauce with brandy and beets. It was called Chicken Cardinale as a reference to the characteristic color that the high priests and cardinals in the Catholic Church usually wear.

The key to success with most of my mother's and my grandma's recipes was always patience. Some recipes require long hours of simmering for meat to be tender and for the flavors to meld together, ending up in a real culinary experience that brings much joy and love to the family. When we would get home from school, and later on in life, from work, we would find all kinds of different dishes that she learned here and there, and she prepared them for the love of the whole family.

Her cakes are memorable. From a simple vanilla cake made with nata, which is the cream on top of fresh milk, to her upside-down pineapple cake, her desserts, bavarois, floating islands, and her mythical bridal cake. She even baked and decorated when I was going to get married. She was a master of preparing all those sweet treats. The love for her family was always her "secret ingredient."

When I was going to get married, the food was prepared by a vendor, but the table of sweets, our family took care of. My oldest cousin from my father's side prepared all kinds of sweets and candies; one of my sisters-in-law also brought some she made herself, and my mother took care of the cake. My aunt flew from Bogota to Quito for the event, bringing with her all the decorations and sugar flowers that another one of my cousins made. It was a beautiful three-tier cake covered in fondant and decorated with magnificent sugar flowers. The taste was beyond words, and the beauty of it was indescribable.

One of my cousins had a flower farm, and he gave us flowers to decorate the church and the venue. My mother's best friend was the one who put my bridal bouquet together. My mother sewed my wedding dress. It was different from everything you could imagine back then. A Roman tunic that was also embroidered by her.

Even though my marriage was a recipe for disaster, my ex-husband used to say that he never saw a bride as beautiful as me that day. Probably because he was still in love with me, but that doesn't matter because everything around that point in time was all about love in the end.

My family is Roman Catholic, and even though I don't consider myself as such anymore, we used to celebrate our children's baptism, first communion, confirmation, and so on. Birthdays were always opportunities to gather and enjoy with family and friends as well.

How wonderful it is to be able to cook and bake for all those souls we love so much. When my kids were very small, they enjoyed their birthday parties with their cousins and friends. I used to prepare everything, from different recipes for the adults coming over to the candies, the ice creams, and their cakes as well. We used to gather at the small park at my parents' building, where they could play different games to finally break the piñata before heading upstairs, where we would all enjoy all kinds of treats.

Through food and throughout several generations, we have been able to demonstrate how much we love and care about our family and friends. Easter was also a time to celebrate. My mother inherited the recipe for *fanesca* from my grandma. This hearty soup that consists of 12 different grains, like the 12 apostles, together with dried cod that has been left in milk to rehydrate overnight, cream, and spices, is served with very tiny fried empanadas, fried sweet plantain, hardboiled eggs sliced thinly, and small balls of fried dough similar to the empanadas. Traditionally, the whole family comes over, and we eat it on Holy Thursday, Friday, and Glory Saturday. For dessert, we usually have figs that have been boiled with brown sugar and cinnamon or rice pudding.

The preparation of the *fanesca* usually takes two days for the ingredients to be ready before the recipe can be put together. There is a lot of love and care in following the recipe, and it also takes a lot of patience, a strong arm to stir it frequently, and lots of time for it to turn out as the most amazing and savory dish you could ever imagine.

When one of my uncles was still alive, we used to invite him over to eat it with us. The best compliment my mother could get was from him, who used to tell her that her version of *fanesca* tasted exactly the same as my grandma's.

As I mentioned before, my father was not really someone who was able to prepare any meal but only some very basic things. Even though he didn't cook, he woke up every single morning before everyone else to prepare breakfast. He knew exactly how we liked our toasts, what to put on them; our coffee at a boiling temperature or lukewarm only. Every single detail imaginable was stored in his head, and that was his duty, which he did relentlessly day after day until his health declined up to the point that he was not able to perform it anymore.

There is no other "secret ingredient" in all those recipes that we have gathered throughout generations and generations other than the love that we have and put into preparing the food, which simply translates into unlimited and unmeasurable love for our family and friends.

No matter the occasion; no matter the celebration; no matter the sadness and deep sorrow, we gather around a table filled with food, and we know that loving each other, being present, and being together is what matters the most.

Long live our love for food and each other!

About Meche Barba

Mercedes, best known as Meche, already felt at a young age that she was quite different from the rest of her family, or so she thought. At the age of 10, she would tell her friends at school that she did not come from this planet but from the stars. She used to do some very clear but still unconscious astral traveling when she was young.

Throughout her life, she has experienced all kinds of what we would call miraculous events and synchronicities, and she is very thankful for the extraordinary gifts and opportunities she has been given. Doing a lot of introspection, working on her family patterns to heal them, and assuming her own faults have defined her as the woman she has become today. In her own words, "It's very tempting to keep playing the role of the victim," but she prefers to snap out of it and create a more peaceful life for herself and everyone else around her as well. She is an empath; she feels others' energy, pain, and suffering. She has always felt the need to help others, so much so that her late friend Francine used to call her Mother Theresa. Countless stories—many of them with a dash of humor, and some other ones to be taken with a pinch of salt—have helped her shape who she is now. She has the gift of channeling some information and messages. Premonitory dreams and clairsentience are also on her menu. Seeing the Spirit Guides of certain people in her mind's eye and describing them in a very accurate way has become very common too.

Her healing path started with Tai Chi classes when she was in her early 20s. Although she no longer is, she became vegetarian back then, learning about macrobiotic foods and much more. Then bioenergetic came along, and she also learned how to see the aura around people, even though she can't see it in colors but only on rare occasions. A fascination with everything that has to do with the energy of the pyramids is tied to her past lives in Egypt, or so she believes. Bit by bit, new opportunities to learn new things come along. Working with crystals, healing with her hands, being able to see the prana, and lighting up her chakras were also added to her repertoire. She loves animals. She can feel their energy, and they are usually drawn to her as well. Trees and plants also vibrate as she puts her hands on top of them. Her life is a permanent work in progress, and sometimes she wishes life would be easier, but she knows that this is the path she chose before she was born.

Meche is also a bestselling author in *Mission Hope, Volume II.*

A Child of God's Mercy

Silifath Houinsou

Love connects, bonds, and brings people with different cultures, beliefs, and understanding together. It is this same love that manifests when two people decide to add another member to their lives. The addition is satiated when we bring another human being to this world. It is called "Birth." Birth is a mystery, a manifestation of the "love" between two individuals, but above and beyond, it is a manifestation of God's love. As women, how do we navigate through the mystery of birth? Believe it or not, it's the most mysterious, yet most magical and beautiful thing we get to experience in our lives. But this experience is portrayed differently from one person to another. How? Well, we all have different body shapes and different health conditions. But if it wasn't for the love of God, would women even be privileged to carry a child? God's love offers a solid foundation for motherhood deeply rooted in compassion that transmits to the baby in our womb. It is a deep correlation that stems from the idea that love breaks obstacles, inviting us to embrace the growing human being inside us. But when things become uneasy, we all wonder if love even exists. Let this chapter serve as a reminder that birth is simply a miracle of God.

It was the end of summer 2017, and we just returned from our mini vacation in Toronto. We spent three magical days experiencing all kinds of things in the city. The view of Niagara Falls alone was magnificent, not to mention the pleasing view of the CN Tower glass floor. It was just amazing to get to change up our routine life in Montreal. We both were happy, and our hearts were full and beyond grateful.

17 days later, I felt unwell. I went to see our family doctor, worried because of the pain I was feeling in my lower abdomen, and that's when I found out I was pregnant. How far along? I wasn't sure. The doctor told my husband and I to go to the ER right away on that day. It wasn't far between the family doctor and the ER, so we headed to the ER, talking about how merciful God is to bring this child into our world. I saw my husband's face lighting up like a breathtaking sunset at the top of a quiet ocean.

We waited a few hours to see a doctor. Then I was told I was miscarrying a 12-week pregnancy—news that was very hard to swallow. How did I not even know I was pregnant? I had little to no understanding of this. My husband inched closer to me and said, "Do not blame yourself for this." His face shied off in tranquility. We both were not able to sleep that night, as the pain just got unbearable in the middle of a night that was already silenced by mixed emotions.

A few months later, we were pregnant again, but this time around, it was all well-planned. I took better care of myself, read every book one could think of about a healthy living pregnancy, and was more conscious about my diet. In fact, I had a better understanding of the dos and don'ts of pregnancy that I believed a healthy baby was growing inside me. I had my first and second ultrasound, and everything looked good. At 16 weeks plus three days, my pregnancy became uncomfortable. I remember asking my boss to allow me to work from home that day, but I could barely work, as the pain kept getting stronger. I did not want to go to the ER. I hated the idea so much that my husband had to coax me to go. I refused a couple of times, but after weighing all the options, that was the only place to go. I begrudgingly agreed, as it almost felt like something was seriously not right, and I wasn't sure I could even face that possibility again. So, off we went.

While we were waiting to see a doctor, I felt my heart was falling out of my chest. I cried my heart out for being in this indescribable pain. In fact, at that moment, I hated being pregnant; I hated God; I hated everything I have ever loved, and I blamed myself for allowing this suffering.

Then my husband looked at me and said, "My body is shivering as I see you in so much pain, and there is nothing I can do. I am such an armless man holding only onto hope and faith." His eyes were watering. I looked at him, seeking answers, but it was as though God had set it out to be a storybook. Love is powerful when the pain of one pouring soul transposes to the quietness and solitude of the other person's brain and runs through the veins like a red wine cooling down your hot blood. It was almost like he was feeling it just as I was.

After crying and squishing for almost four hours, I saw the doctor who later did an ultrasound. The baby was OK. I heard the heartbeat. Oh, thank God! Everything looked good, she observed. She then informed me that I had eight fibroids in the uterus, and the biggest one was sitting right at the edge, causing the pain. I was admitted for the night. They put me on some pain killers, and I slept it off. It was around 4 a.m., and I felt like I needed to use the restroom. I went, came back, and slept some more. I woke up, went to the restroom again, and I found myself in blood. I went to the secretary immediately and informed the nurse. The doctor called me in for a checkup. "You have lost the baby," she said with a sigh. I asked, "Why? My baby was there. I saw the baby during the ultrasound. I heard the heartbeat. You told me everything looked good. Then what happened? What did you give me to drink? Why did I lose my baby?" She answered, "Once there are fibroids, there will always be miscarriages." Now, that didn't faze me at all because she had an aura that confused me totally; she was already very negative in her comments right from the moment she entered the examination room, with a facial expression that conveyed a message of racism and no empathy. But one thing is for sure: she is not God.

The doctor removed the baby from my uterus and asked to run some genetic tests. She wrote her report, from which I would later learn she felt like crying. She sent my file to a specialist at another hospital; it is a clinic specialized in treating women with fibrosis diseases.

They kept me at the hospital for a few hours and sent me home without painkillers. I was still in a lot of pain.

We decided to visit another ER at a newly built hospital in the same city. To our surprise, this ER wasn't that crowded, so I was seen by the house nurse very quickly, followed by the doctor a few minutes later. I explained that I had just miscarried a baby and that I was there because I had a lot of pain. He accessed my file and called a second doctor in for advice. They both looked very professional and knew what they were doing. They searched for information on every possible medication I could take and consulted with each other before giving me anything. I was admitted for the night, and many tests were done. The next morning, I felt better, so we were released after seeing the doctor for a final checkup. This hospital had just become my favorite. I could not have asked for a better one, and I would later learn why. That was the same hospital my file was sent to. They had mentioned that they would call me for an appointment.

I waited over six months with no return or reply. My hubby kept insisting I see another gynecologist in the meantime. I first refused but finally acquiesced to his request.

We were both very excited about this new appointment, but frustration set in very quickly because this doctor did not run any tests on me. Nothing! It was a complete waste of time explaining why I was there, I thought! He just said, "Looking at the situation, surely the fibroids are still there. No need for further checkups. I will give you a prescription for three months of use." Then I asked, "This medication is not compatible with pregnancy; does it have any side effects?" He responded, "The only thing that could be a cause for concern is that it can affect your liver; so, you need to do a blood test every month."

I told my husband that I was not going to take any kind of treatment that could affect my liver. I went back home and threw the medication in the dustbin, asserting, "If God wants this for us, He will surely make it happen," and I never looked back. Two weeks later, on August 7, 2018, I found out I was already seven weeks pregnant. Hubby was still asleep when I woke him up with the news. He couldn't believe it. He asked me if I was sure about the news. Not that he isn't a believer; he was unassuming.

I finally got the call from the specialized clinic which booked me in for an appointment. By the appointment date, I was 11 weeks pregnant. The doctor said, "You have eight fibroids in the uterus, and there is typically an 80% chance of losing the baby once there are fibroids. Plus, you miscarried twice before, so we are going to declare your pregnancy as high risk." With tears in my eyes, I replied, "OK. God is in control." My file was immediately sent to another specialized obstetrician at the same clinic, who instantly requested a 12-week checkup.

I saw this obstetrician every two weeks. He urged me not to take any medication without his consent, not even vitamins. I wouldn't say I was lucky but loved enough by God who made the way.

16 weeks: I woke up in blood. Eyes in tears, I thought to myself, *Here we go again!* My next appointment was set to be the following week. I can't go to the birthing center before 18 weeks. Lord! I refused to go to the ER. I refused to hear "You're having a miscarriage" again. I kept saying, "Lord, I am Your child. Don't let this story follow me." Hubby asked, "What should we do? I answered, "Nothing! I am not going anywhere. I am going to sit here and let God handle this one." He did not force me this time to go to the ER; it was almost like the universe was listening. I sat all day and kept praying to God for a miracle. One of my brothers, Chiam, who is against medicinal toxicomania and promotes healing through meditation and canalization of our body parts had asked me to meditate. Chiam had played a very big role in this pregnancy right from the beginning. Just as the roots of a tree are hidden underground and play a central role in its existence and health, there is a subtle energy system influencing the physical and mental health of every human being.

Chiam's understanding of the anatomy and functioning of the energetic body that surrounds and interpenetrates us enables him to take action to restore the body's energetic balance through healing protocols that promote overall well-being. During this meditation, you concentrate on the median of your forehead and visualize each part of your body, which in acupuncture is numbered and represents a point. I meditated, focusing on healing through my body using those points. I kid you not, this exercise is very powerful. I did it all day nonstop. The next morning, the blood had stopped. Honey, that was the miracle I had asked for! Please do not ever let medical history follow you. If I had gone to the ER that day, history would have followed me. They would have thought to themselves, *She is losing a third one.*

19 weeks: My doctor informed me that my cervix was opening, and if it continued, we would lose the baby. We could have done a cerclage if this was discovered before 16 weeks, but at this point, it was not viable. I was thinking, *Hmmm, so what now?* The doctor said, "We are going to put you on bed rest. You need to stop doing any house chores; no walking, unless from bed to the bathroom. Come back in two weeks for another checkup. If your cervix opens more, we will have to keep you at the hospital for the remaining months of the pregnancy." Two weeks later, on December 13th, I went back for the check-up. The doctor said, "Your cervix has closed back." Hugh! Hallelujah!!

32 weeks: As if everything already was not enough, they said I had a marginal cord insertion. *What is that?* I wondered. The doctor said, "So, this is a situation whereby the insertion of the cord is supported by very little placental tissues, making food transition and oxygen to the baby take longer, which can lead to complications later in pregnancy." At that point, my brain just stopped working. My husband proclaimed, "Dieu est grand," meaning "God is good." The doctor further said, "We need to monitor this very carefully for the next coming weeks." All I could think of at that point was, *Lord, You can't give up on me now.* On this day, I remember a conversation with one of the other pregnant ladies while we were waiting to see our OB-GYN. The woman asked me who my doctor was, and I told her who it was. She asked me how I got this doctor and

how I got on a waiting list. Apparently, he specialized in high-risk pregnancies. "People say he is God," she said. I answered her with a little laugh, "Well, it is because only God can look after my pregnancy." She replied that she could see I'm a believer.

Eight months plus one week, the pain started from nowhere. At the birthing center, my husband kept saying to the nurse that we still had three more weeks to go and asked the nurse to please give us some pain medications so that we could go home. The doctor told us, "You're considered full-term at 37 weeks!" Plus, my contractions were just two minutes apart. He said that they were admitting me for delivery right then!

On March 20, 2019, I delivered a beautiful baby boy amidst all complications. I got tired and could not push anymore; the baby started breathing low. Three more doctors were called in during delivery, to name the least. God was hard at work, preparing each and every one of the doctors and nurses for this day that only He knew was coming. If I had used that prescription from the gynecologist who didn't test me, my big boy wouldn't be here. Perhaps, if I had gone to the ER the third time, he wouldn't be here either. See, it's beyond the understanding of mankind. I named him Mumiah, meaning "God, end of all things." With this child, God ended my suffering and selfless belief toward birth. Life hasn't been the same since then.

During my postpartum visit, after delivery, I asked the doctor if he thought I should go for surgery to remove the fibroids. He looked at me with staggering eyes and replied, "No, not when they are inside the uterus. Have you ever heard of women who removed their fibroids or cysts but still can't have kids? If you go under the knife, you risk damaging or losing part or even the whole of your uterus. Do you want to have more kids?" I responded that I did. Then he told me not to go for surgery. "When you finish making your kids, you can remove them if you wish. But I can assure you with my 30-plus years in practice, you are not going to have easy pregnancies, and if you do make it to term, it will be a great addition to your family. Congratulations!"

A friend of mine had briefed me about hormonal IUDs and how effective they are for her. I asked the doctor if I could get it. He told me that it doesn't work with fibrosis. We shook hands, and I said, "Thank you very much for everything, Doctor God," remembering what the other pregnant woman had told me in the lobby.

In everything, God has the last say. But above and beyond, two things always work together, love and faith. Love covers us in this deep connection that transcends barriers. Faith reflects our belief inspired by God's love. Working together, they both align our aspirations with goals that embody the true essence of each of us. To say that God's love didn't prevail in all this is absolutely incorrect. To the women all over the world who can relate to my story, I pray you get to know the awesome God that I know and that you get to experience His love and mercy that takes us all from glory to glory.

Today, I am a mom of two beautiful boys, which I never thought was going to be possible, not even in a million years. I cherish motherhood profoundly and never take anything for granted. Proverbs 4:18, "The path of the righteous is like the morning sun, shining ever brighter till the full light of day."

With a grateful heart …

About Silifath Houinsou

 Silifath Houinsou was born in Porto-Novo, Republic of Benin, in 1989. She is a serious, responsible, and sensible citizen who loves to live in the moment without feeling forced to keep moving forward. She graduated from a private school at the University of Benin and left for South Africa to continue her education.

After completing her bachelor's degree in finance from the University of South Africa, she moved to Canada in 2017. She believes we are all capable of achieving great things, but we each need a safe place to explore the blockages we all experience that prevent our forward momentum and growth.

Currently pursuing a certification in accounting and finance at the School of Continuing Studies of the University of McGill, she is excited to join projects where cooperation is based on everyone's goodwill.

Heartbeat Rhythms

———

Stephanie Mangels Watson

HEARTBEAT: *the vital center or driving impulse.*

Why am I still here? I wasn't supposed to make it. The thoughts ring in my head.

God kept me around for a reason. I had to find out what that reason was…

I recently had not one but two transformational changes of heart. I am learning to listen to my new heartbeats and now have a NEW life *heartbeat rhythm* stronger than ever through the healing power of self-love. This is a story about facing adversity and reworking my life to come out better than ever on the other side. Refining and re-aligning my talents and strengths to enhance all aspects of life … to truly live and love every minute of it!

I have always lived my life a little outside of the proverbial box, or at least healthily pushed those boundaries. Not enough to get into trouble but enough to make things interesting. I live on the edges of whatever "box" I find myself in—taking the path less traveled, sometimes making my own way, and reflecting on atypical solutions and visions. All the while striving to make the world a better place for all. And making my path my own, finding the 'give,' I then capitalize on things in fresh and innovative ways, making it a little bigger, a little better, than before. Some call it judicious risk-taking. I call it a way of life. It's just how I think. It's how I honor myself, but I did not always love myself. This way of life helped me in the past and has now assisted me immensely on my current journey toward complete love of self and listening to my heart.

Through my judicious risk-taking, I also go all in! I don't know how to do things part way or halftime, especially when it comes to something I am trying, building, implementing, and/or managing. I go deep into projects, relationships, initiatives, work, people, and so on. I think deeply, process continuously, and believe fiercely. But, back then, I did not always pay attention to my *heartbeat rhythm*, my center. Until recently …

This story is about listening to one's heart and *heartbeat rhythm*, both in real terms and in learning to love yourself, so you don't lose yourself in physical and metaphorical terms. It's about loving yourself enough to truly listen to and then take on and own those new rhythms that many of us ignore, push aside, and don't care to know. I was guilty of doing all three.

Currently and since 2001, I have run a consulting business in the metro Atlanta, GA, area that helps non-profits level up in services and programming, funding, partnerships, and strategic positioning. I call it "nonprofit navigation." My heart and love of work have always been aligned with those in need and those who face inequities. I never thought that I would become a small business owner, as I just wanted to use my master's degree in social work planning and administration to better the world and have a flexible schedule doing it. I started this business a bit by accident. In those days, my *heartbeat rhythm* was tied to the school calendar, being on PTA at school, and being room-mom in each of my three boys' classrooms.

When my twins started preschool, I thought, *Let me just do something from home—a bit nontraditional.* So, I started consulting work with one non-profit for about 3–4 hours a week. Never did I dream what it would turn into. I now know it was the launch of what is currently becoming my legacy and part of my center (my heart) because, again, I can't do something just part-time, let alone only 3–4 hours per week! Be careful what you ask for. I continue to grow. It was and is glorious! But something was missing—there were no guideposts or guardrails. What I realize now is that what I was lacking was taking care of myself, of my center, and self-care and self-love. I hope to explain my path in a way that helps others look at their *heartbeat rhythm* and journey toward loving themselves.

Nonetheless, in pushing those traditional edges, I struggled internally and personally as my business grew. Struggled with where the boundaries were between work and home and personal life and professional life. You see, my career "work" IS me. It is my heart. In pushing those soft edges to advance and grow, boundaries would often get fuzzy and bleed into each other. Helping, assisting, and counseling organizations is my nature, and I fully embrace doing so. Maybe you feel something in your life is the same way—a hobby, your career, a particular subject you continually educate yourself on, or certain relationships—something that you get engrossed in, and it takes over.

Even when boundaries dissolved into each other, I kept working and kept striving. After all, I *was* making a difference. I *was* helping those who help people—the marginalized, the forgotten, those without a voice. Deep in the trenches of poverty and inequality, I was "saving" those who could not or did not know how to save themselves. However, was I working on saving myself, listening to me and my body? Over and over, my *heartbeat rhythm* would become rapid, frantic, and over-taxed. I worked with a counselor, a career coach, my life partner, and close friends to help ease the load—one that quickly became a burden a multitude of times over throughout those 10–12 years. My life counselors and I would come up with a plan that would help for a while, and then things would pile up again. My *heartbeat rhythm* was out of whack, unbalanced, and sometimes would throw me into a tailspin. Each time, I would say, "There has to be a better way—a better path."

Working through COVID

Then, in 2020, COVID hit and threw us all, the nation, and the world into turmoil. Philanthropic work was more vital than ever, and I was stretched almost to my breaking point without a guiding center. As I took on more and more, I was in over my head, in too deep, and being pulled in even deeper. But my thoughts were, "I AM making huge differences, nevertheless." Right? However, I suffered more. My self-love and self-care were non-existent. My *heartbeat rhythm* strained, and I huffed and puffed. I was trying to be "the hero" to turn my clients, and many other organizations, to be COVID-facing and to be a part of the solution. I was successful on many of those levels, but I deteriorated, and so did my *heartbeat rhythm*. I pictured myself swooping in to save the day, to make things better. I struggled continually with the question "What is my part to play in all of this?" Buried, drowning that Spring of 2020 after four months of billing three times as many hours as I typically do (how does anyone do that?), it was imperative for me to let off the gas. I did … I refreshed for about two weeks—in a daze for that first week. I needed to heed the adage "Put your mask on first." (Particularly pertinent to the pandemic times.) Now, I know in my mind that to continue and help anyone, you must ensure you help yourself first.

After those two weeks in May of 2020, I told myself that I finally needed to pay attention to my heartbeat rhythm and not bury myself. I laid the groundwork with my support system once again and took a deep breath with more determination to do better and consider myself in the equation. But I dove back in, and before I knew it, I was back at it. I felt like I learned nothing or at least didn't heed warning signs and signals. With my mental health throwing up flares to slow down, take on less, and practice self-care and self-love, I forged ahead "knowing" I had great things just down the road.

The Event

December of 2022 was one of the busiest months I remember. The holidays always are, but these were the first since the pandemic had shut things down, and everyone was coming out of isolation. During the first part of the month, I realized I had 11 events to go to in 10 days! Wait, what? More events than there were days! My daily *heartbeat rhythm* quickened again. But weren't we all just catching up from the last 2.5 years of shutdowns, distancing, virtual meetings, and more? I convinced myself it was OK. I'd be OK. And then life caught up with me!

Getting ready for that 11th event proved almost fatal but, in many ways, saved my life! I was 54 at the time. In a rush to get ready; trying to find the tickets; looking up where we were to park; figuring out the mingling timeframe before the event, the show, the after party … (whew, makes me tired just writing that list). All of a sudden, I felt like I had to sit down. Exhausted and out of breath, I needed a breather. And then it hit me!

A ton of bricks landed on my chest, and I fell over on the couch with a pain so intense that I saw stars—it took my breath away. I could hear in the distance, as if far away, my life partner saying, "Honey, Steph, honey, are you OK?!" But yet he was standing in the same room. I faded in and out, and I heard him say, "I'm calling 911 unless you tell me not to." The pain was powerful and impacted my thought processes. I couldn't breathe. I blacked in and out. I heard him yell over the phone, "You need to get someone here now! She needs someone here now!"

I faintly heard my purse and bag spilling on the countertops as he searched for the medications I take. He raced to me, handed me three small pills, and said, "Here, take these." They were low-dose aspirin. I took them, even though I felt like they would come back up. They didn't. I heard him go out the front door to signal the first responders. I lay on the couch, clutching my chest, panting, writhing, kicking my leg against the couch cushions, and screaming, "It's too much!" I was in and out of consciousness. Then the paramedics arrived, loaded me into the ambulance, and told my partner not to follow them because they were going as fast as they could. He had to meet us there. The drive was fuzzy and distorted.

Wheeling into the ambulance bay at the hospital, there were five to six medical staff waiting for me to be unloaded. The pain had mostly subsided because they gave me life-saving medications on the way. One started to push the gurney; one was feeding liquids into an IV; one was giving me some oral meds; one was undressing me to get me ready for what was next; and two others were racing around, preparing my way … for what? I didn›t know. The paramedic had said to me, "We are taking you the fastest way to the hospital. Your partner will meet us there. You are having severely abnormal *heart rhythms*. They will be waiting for us." Those words kept churning over (and still do) in my head. After a short medical history, I was taken to another room, where I faintly heard voices, soft but direct. The pain was much less by this point. I was exhausted but alive and aware. I knew there were three people in the room with me. I felt safe, comforted, and finally gave in to «sleep.»

Then … sometime later, feeling groggy and a bit tingly … I struggled to open my eyes. Fluttering and then closing again. Fluttering … and I could make out a black and white x-ray screen with what looked like a fat needle and thread going through a network of ribbon pathways. My eyes closed, fluttering again; I saw the screen once more and realized I couldn't move my right arm to turn over. My eyes closed—drifting again. Fluttering open one more time, my eyes focused, and over me stood a peaceful gentleman dressed all in white, with one arm tucked behind his back, and his other gently resting on my arm. It was the doctor that saved my life—just one of the angels that day. "Stephanie, can you hear me? You are OK," he said. My eyes closed. He said, "Stephanie, everything is OK. Are you with us?" Was I?

I forced my eyes open and looked at the gentleman; he was framed in a white aura from behind (they had to keep the lights low, it seemed). He was the doctor on call and happened to be one of the top cardiologists in the state! And by the way, I was taken to the closest hospital to where I was at the time—one of the top ones for cardiac care in GA! I found out these two facts later. There are no coincidences.

The doctor said, "Stephanie, you had a heart attack. It was in your left anterior descending artery—the LAD—and it was 99% blocked. We got it. You are going to be OK."

I realized later that I had survived what they call the "widow maker" heart attack. It was a miracle. It happened on 12/12/2022. My partner saved my life by acting so quickly. I am so grateful to him! What if he hadn›t been there? Again, there are no coincidences. Why did I survive? Why was I kept on Earth?

Early Processing

In the days to come and in my early processing of this event, I had the deep realization that my *heartbeat rhythm* and self-love had gotten so much out of alignment that it almost killed me. My three boys would have had no mother; my soulmate would have been without a partner; and my 89-year-old father would have survived losing another of his three girls (my youngest sister passed several years before). These facts settled deep into my bones.

As I mentioned at the beginning of this passage, in theory, medically, logically, I was not supposed to be here. Most do not make it. I did. Now, my journey toward self and love of myself is about finding out why I was spared and kept here on Earth. What was my new life and my new *heartbeat rhythm* supposed to be? What did this experience teach me? And how did the power of love, my love for me and my true center, see me through?

Current Processing

One year later, I am writing this and still processing. It's been a year of a lot of hard work! A different kind of work, though—on my two heartbeats. One is my *physical heartbeat*, which is connected to my journey to "better health" and overall well-being. I make the best choices I can when eating, get more rest and sleep, and engage in a life exercise and movement routine. I lost 35 pounds and spent more time with family and friends in my leisure time. I re-evaluated EVERYTHING. And I mean everything

… The other is to get my life's *heartbeat rhythm* back in alignment with self-love, self-care, and what I am *supposed* to be doing (a different type of center or heart)—what I was kept on this earth to do. One of making conscious decisions to live life on purpose with authenticity, and intentionality, and to truly show me compassionate love.

Journeying forward, I am now stronger and more vital, and all areas of my life have been enhanced—family, relationships, work and career, friendships, recreation, and faith. I have discovered a new *heartbeat rhythm*, one centered on self. Not selfishly but being good to myself so that I can be good to others.

Currently, my health numbers (bloodwork, blood pressure, cholesterol, A1C) are all stellar. Physically, my heart is currently back to 100% functioning—that hardly ever happens. The doctor said, "It's another miracle!" The first is that I survived. Many things lined up that day to ensure that I did. Once again, there are no coincidences. I call it "divine intervention."

Additionally, through hard work in my adversity, other qualities are currently top-notch as well, such as my critical thinking and problem-solving skills—many of which I use in my life, work, and career. My interactions with my partner, my kids, my family and friends, and my clients are superlative and unsurpassed. My heart attack was a blessing in disguise. One that allowed for the power of self-love to emerge and bloom.

Finding Purpose

Due to this developing self-love, I have found that I can see things more clearly now. I felt like I was close to living out my purpose before my heart attack, but I now KNOW there was too much clutter, too much "stuff" blocking the way to truly do so. My heart attack allowed me to clear away the blockages (literally and figuratively) and the overgrowth to give me a better view of how God wants me to live my life and my "why."

Mentally, emotionally, and spiritually, it changed me—transformed my way of life and my way of thinking—and made a new path for me. One of intentionality, clarity, and caring for self, and one closer to my true and real *heartbeat rhythm*. It permitted me to discard old ways, thoughts, and patterns that were not serving me. I am currently paring away things from home life, work, career, client work, and saying "no" more and more often (always a challenge) to those things that do not fulfill me.

I am allowing myself time to think, *Where do I WANT to go? What is my true core desire? What IS my vital center? How do I care for and love myself through all that life throws at me?* And my favorite question now that I ask myself with almost every decision is, *Does 'this' serve me? Does it get me closer to the life I WANT to live and to the love of life itself that I am creating?*

I had a *physical* AND *metamorphic change* of heart. It's hard stuff— no one said it wouldn't be. But I know I will continue to be happier and healthier in the long run. My heart, my vital center, will continue to grow stronger. Since I live more deeply fulfilled following every heartbeat, not only will I thrive, but also, my family and the people and communities I love and serve will allow for that new *heartbeat rhythm* to prevail in all areas of my life.

When I listen to my heartbeats, divinely driven, I believe … I very much *know* I hear transformational things … I hear beautiful love-filled whispers of my legacy … I must follow those whispers … use them as my guide … my heart … carefully listening and intentionally responding. My heart has changed; my life and path are more fully defined, and the world is better for it. I was doing so much, and perhaps a bunch of "wrong" things, because the world and society said so far too many things that my heart literally *broke*. To piece it back together, I had to do something radically different. And now, I am!

New Heartbeat Rhythm

Just a few months ago, in September of 2023, my life changed again. This time, my *heartbeat rhythm* guided me in a direction that had been playing in the background for the last 10 years within my world of work. This directed me toward the path of a renewed essential center related to what I now believe is part of that legacy. Because of the work on myself that I had done over the previous year, I had an epiphany that literally shook me to my core but was more in alignment with my center than ever.

Since my heart attack, I have been asking God to direct that path with some very distinct life choices, and He gave me the answers loud and clear. It came from listening to the vision within my heart. Without the past 9–10 months, I would not have heard the answers. Is this what self-love looks like? Is this what God is trying to teach me? I think so! Since then, and after several realizations about living in self-love, I am on a bigger and better path than ever before. My "broken" heart ultimately led me to them. "I" am is now part of this life's equation because I ensure it includes "me" in every move I make. The very in-depth and all-consuming work that I did that did not allow "me" room before and almost ended me has now become life-giving again. I am seeing things through a new lens.

Through purposeful and quiet listening and caring for myself, I was able to see a clear vision for my work that does not take over my boundaries! I'm telling you, it has washed over and drenched me. The endless fighting with myself—the roadblocks—were eliminated within my mind and heart, and my direction was clear. I don't even know what I was fighting ... I am now content and have deep peace within this—self-love is evident.

After getting lost one weekend and following a road detour to see my partner, answers came to me. They tumbled into my head and gave me the direction that I so desperately needed. In light of this self-love, I earnestly asked God to guide my path. The answers revolve around listening to myself, following my gut, and attending to my heart. My health events led me to this in-depth understanding and then to the self-love that I had been denying.

When I finally figured out where I was physically that night after driving through several neighborhoods, I pulled out onto the main highway from my "detour," and the hospital where I received treatment for my heart attack was right in front of me! Remember, there are no coincidences. I still don't know how I got there that night; I was lost. But now I know exactly why.

Tears glazed my cheeks, and teardrops stained my shirt, but I knew. I just knew that I had discovered a significant piece of my puzzle—and my pathway to amazing things that my sister spoke of (see the end of this passage to understand). I was in a surreal daze the rest of the night and exhausted the next day but all in a good way.

Akin Feelings

Currently, the way I describe all of this is that it holds the same feelings I had when my mom died. My mom died of complications due to cancer over 12 years ago after seven long years of fighting it. These same feelings of peace and being right with the world were the same type of «knowing" feelings that washed over me then. Knowing that it was the right time for her to go and knowing she was going to be with God.

Later that evening, that Friday night of my last epiphany, I said "Hi, Mom! I see you; I feel you." I wonder if it is her telling me that it's OK. I guess it is. She is saying, «If this is what will make you happy, let's do it!" I experienced a feeling of peace and contentment with a deep cleansing sigh and then calm.

There is so much more to the story. Far too much to outline here. Telling my story helps me continue to heal emotionally and mentally—the physical has already been restored, and then some! It strengthens my resolve to not only continue my life of intention and taking time for myself but also to live out my vision, my purpose, and my love. To follow this NEW strong and vital *heartbeat rhythm*—both of them. It feels right! So right! What I experienced was God's love and plan unfolding and directing my life path. I just know it.

In Closing

I had major transformative changes of heart—two of them. Both gave me my new life and gave me extraordinary purpose and direction. Both have made me better, more whole, than before. Both provided imprints of the "power of love."

My sister told me, "God wanted you to do something amazing. Now, go find out what that is." That was my charge. With my mind and body now strengthened, I am well on my way with a renewed "driving impulse" and a new re-birth filled with self-love and new amazing possibilities. I am physically healed and sound. I will continue to focus on overall health and well-being as well as self-love and the life-giving nature of my work.

My journey is far from over, but I AM on the right path. My heart is strong, and my center is, too. My decisions and choices are clear. My soul is refreshed and emboldened. Again, my heart attack was a blessing in disguise. I am traveling in the right direction. I feel a loving, renewed sense of purpose—mighty, healthy, vibrant, and ready to take on the vision and my life's charge!

I hope not to miss one heartbeat now. Listening to the two new *heartbeat rhythms* God has given me.

With love,
Stephanie

About Stephanie Mangels Watson

Stephanie was born in Connecticut right outside of New York City and moved to South Carolina in high school. Ever since, she has lived in the southeast US and considers Atlanta, GA, her home. Stephanie received her Master of Social Work, Administration, and Planning degree from Virginia Commonwealth University (VCU) and her bachelor's degree from Furman University in Early and Elementary Education, Special Education, and Studio Art. Stephanie is a lifelong learner, a connector, a designer, a mentor, and an avid pursuer of her visions and dreams. She believes deeply in the goodness that resides in all people and is passionate about equity.

She loves working with nonprofit organizations that are changing the world. Deeply involved in the community and with the organizations she works with, she loves working with both leaders and program directors alike and loves putting theory into action and the intersection of program models and service implementation. She has served the Social Work/Social Services program and administration field since 1991, offering time-tested and innovative services and consultation in non-profit growth and program development as well as grant strategy, funder relations, and proposal writing.

She has an extensive working knowledge of non-profit and governmental agencies, organizations, and systems and integrates it with in-depth best practices and comprehensive service delivery. Her niche is working with children and families, child welfare, child abuse prevention, mental health and substance abuse, homelessness, public health, domestic violence, and educational entities; she often cross-pollinates programming and practices. Since 2010, she has raised more than $60 million for her clients from funders big and small, designed a multitude of strategic plans, initiated and cultivated countless successful partnerships, and designed and implemented hundreds of program models.

She is currently writing a book and is interested in pursuing her doctorate and traveling the world. In her spare time, she spends time going on big and small adventures with her life partner, scrapbooking and creating memory books for others, walking, reading, working jigsaw puzzles and creative projects, connecting with friends, and raising her three active boys.

The Auntie Chronicles:
Loving Without Limits

——

Maria Lehtman

This story is a kaleidoscope of my experiences as an auntie and a fairy godmother. My chapter is dedicated to other aunties and women without children. These are my thoughts as they were during the time I had them. I want you to know that I have lived my life to the fullest. And I have no regrets. Love yourself as you are.

Meeting the Little Prince

Where lies the boundary between womanhood and motherhood? Our ability to love is what truly defines us. The Universe showers us with love whenever our hearts are true. In the infinite light, there is no us and them. One day you will see what I see. The beauty of motherhood is all around us.
—Maria Lehtman

The year 2013

For months now, a little boy had been entering my dreams. He appeared in different ages and moods, sometimes silent, energetic, funny, and at times in need of help. One night, I woke up at dawn to a dream about Christmas and a boy underneath the tree. I called the little boy to me.

Soon after, it was late in the evening, and I was lying down in my hotel room—one of the many hotel nights traveling in Europe from one business meeting to another. I used my limited pass time scanning emails and learning astronomy and science. I would watch one video after another, trying to determine what theories best fit the quantum healing practices or explain them. Not that I expected our science to be very far in clarifying multi-dimensional energy healing principles.

Then I felt it, rather than saw it. Someone was standing next to me.

"He would like to spend a little time with you," a voice in my mind spoke.

"Please, it would mean a lot to him. You are one of the few people he can connect with directly. He would like you to sing to him. May we give him to you for a little while? We will stay right here?"

It was odd because I saw the child as the full-grown spirit that he was and the child at the same time. You could call it child practice mode. To the spirit, it feels as if you had just been born again. I set my iPad aside and opened my arms to invite the little boy with my healing energy. I felt him in my arms as he lay on the down-filled duvet. His aura was light and calm like a child's sheltered dream.

After a while, I gathered myself and began singing. The same songs my mother used to sing to me at night. They helped me to fall asleep. Finally, my voice cracked, and tears started welling in my eyes. I loved the spirit boy, but something in him unraveled all the emotions I had entombed inside me. It was as if all the possible futures in my past had opened to me. Forgotten memories filled my mind. I felt overwhelmingly sad about the dreams that would never come true.

I signaled his teachers, and they lifted the little spirit boy from my lap. They thanked me and disappeared as quickly as they had arrived. I was alone again, trying to compose myself. It was not that I desired to have children of my own, but it was like someone had touched the cords of motherhood inside me. I had not expected to feel such deep love—sometimes life hands us healing that we do not know we even lost.

The Dream Family

Hush, little one; the world is so large. Dream about flowery meadows and dips into pristine lakes. Keep the laughter in your voice and sunshine in your eyes. —Maria Lehtman

"I can so see it!" she says brightly. "You will have two children, a boy and a girl. They are smartly dressed like you, and you will have two dogs—Dalmatians, of course—and you work for the United Nations."

This was the vision my schoolmates had of my adulthood. I loved it, although it seemed very far for a 14-year-old girl. I saw the pretty two children standing in the garden in cute matching sailor outfits. (Don't ask me; I don't know why. Perhaps because it was the thing in old photos, white and marine blue sailor outfits.) The sun was shining, and the dogs were sniffing out new scents on the grass. No one ever mentioned the father. Perhaps he was the one taking the photo.

In my childhood, one of the few ways of making some pocket money was babysitting. A known charity organization, The Mannerheim League for Child Welfare, in Finland, offers a certification program for babysitters to learn basic childcare. I took the course and got the certificate, which allowed me to also be in their pool of babysitters. We lived in a small community at the time, so word soon got around, and I had opportunities frequently.

When I turned 15, my mother organized for me to stay with a Finnish-Swedish family in Stockholm. I looked after four children, the oldest of them only 10 years old. It was a hefty education for a young woman. I woke up early in the morning to the noise when all four were "playing" the piano at the same time. I had taken piano lessons for several years, so I started to play and sing, draw, and spend creative time with the children. They soon learned that the piano was a useful instrument and that paper and pens were magic waiting to happen. One by one, they ran to my room, asking me to draw anything, from princesses to trucks. It was fun, although I missed home very much.

Years later, I met the eldest girl, a beautiful young woman. She approached me and said, "I started taking piano lessons after you left; I still play the piano." I was so happy. I felt like Mary Poppins. In a small way, I influenced a child to love music. It was more than I could hope for. Creativity has always been my vehicle of love.

It seems like a lifetime ago. Sometimes I wonder who that girl was, where she came from, and where she went. Very few people realize that I have spent time with children from very early on. I have two little sisters. I am fully aware that I was far from a role model to them—I played pranks on them, guilty, but I loved them.

I took my babysitting role seriously. The movies where the teenage girl sits on the phone, gossiping with her friends, or is chilling out, chatting with her boyfriend on the mobile, could not be further from my babysitting experiences. I was committed 100% when I spent time with the little ones. I wish I had known what I know now when I was young. I would have spent more time supporting my little sisters. We had a very dysfunctional family, and it got a lot worse when I left home, even though my parents eventually divorced. I did not know the truth at the time. My mother never told me how ill she was—she lied about her condition. My younger sisters could not tell me how vulnerable and alone they felt. A child assumes the truth is there for everyone to see.

Remember: Whatever you decide for yourself, be honest. Carry the responsibility of whatever you choose your family life to look like. Cherish the life you are given. Steer your love to where your passion is. You cannot mend the past, but you can address it.

The Lost Love

You left me my heart
Can Love feel cold
And heavy like steel

The anguish boils like an ocean
Swirling in my bizarre world

I walk to the shoreline

Powerless I kneel on the beach
The tears are like shards of sand
Jagged and dry
They ran out long ago

The blood blinded by hate
Rushes through me quicker
And stronger
The water lashes at my back
The wind pulls apart my clothing

Come and collect your heart
Take mine away as well
I only wish to be like the sand
Swirling between the wind and the water

—Maria Lehtman (Oct 24, 1994)

The year 1992

I was 20 years old and sitting at the church. My first love had died a year ago at the age of 21 by his own hand, although, at the time, I thought he died in a car accident. The congregations we belonged to at the time were caring but judgmental. It would have been shameful if the word had gotten around that he had killed himself; so, the truth was hidden, even from me. I watched as patriarchs one after another stepped behind the podium to testify to the importance of family, eternal bliss, responsibilities, and faith. I no longer remember what they said. All I heard was the word *family* repeated again and again. The more they talked about family, the more stressed out I got.

Finally, it was too much for me. I closed the door behind me and left the religion. I had my own faith. It did not include broken, dysfunctional parents beaming in front of the congregation, speaking as if they did not have the same problems everyone else had. I knew enough from my own family that everyone expected a façade over the truth. I felt that I had no eternal family, nor did I even want one. I had a broken childhood that nothing could fix. I had a crushed heart that felt like dried and shattered rose leaves. A half of me disappeared the day I heard my beloved had died. I was determined not to build more chaos in this world.

If you had settled into my mind back then, you would have heard a tick-tock-tick-tock ... a counter. It was so loud that it filled my mind 24/7. You would have felt that in my soul sat a timebomb. You would have held your breath so that it would not go off. How could someone live with a bomb inside them? I can tell you that it was not easy. It took me two years to dismantle the bomb so that it did not go off and take me with it. When my dear friend died, my whole world became focused on my survival and finding security.

Considering everything I had experienced, I decided never to have children. My hormones had already made that decision for me, but adding to that was my genealogy—all the potentially inherited illnesses and my mother's struggle to retain pregnancies and her life. She had altogether five miscarriages that I am aware of. Mentally and physiologically, I would have struggled against a tide that was not on my side. My decision was solid, grounded in my self-awareness and what I anticipated from the future. And let me tell you, I was not wrong. I was extremely mature, considering my age. Ready to take responsibility for my actions and inaction.

Remember: Love yourself enough to let you heal. No one else knows your pain or the time it takes to recover.

The Soulmate 0.2

A thought
A single thought
Like a crystal clear snowflake
Can change one moment

Toward light
Hope
Love
Gather many
And the world
Changes her frequency

—*Maria Lehtman (2023)*

The year 1996

Four years have gone by since I lost my heart to someone who returned to the stars. I have finally met someone I love. It is a different kind of love, but I feel it in my core. I am afraid of marriage. It reminds me of institutions rather than a love story with a beautiful happily ever after. I know I will not relive my parents' marriage; I chose differently. However, there is still a great fear. I told him I could not have children. It was not only that I was not physically capable, but I also did not want to even try. I love children. I work with children, and I cherish the moments with my older sister's lively and lovely trio. They always make me laugh and feel joyful. What I am missing is a passion to have a child of my own. I feel that this need never existed in me. I also do not trust myself to manage the strain on my body. I have migraines and fibromyalgia aches. Without painkillers, I would not manage my workdays.

It was a blessing that my husband-to-be accepted this, and despite how he enjoyed playing with children, he did not push the agenda. So, I went back to church one last time—this time, to get married. Not eternally; I felt content loving someone here, in this lifetime. Let the other side worry about what happens in the great beyond.

We travel to the Alps every winter once or twice for snowboarding. I love the scenery and the quiet. There is a calmness in the mountains, very different from the ocean; it speaks to me. Perhaps it is the grounding force. The elements are grander than anything we humans could build.

Sitting in the ski lift makes me feel as if I am flying across the scenery.

It is a busy day in Engelberg (The Angel Mountain). Locals and tourists are crowding the ski station, and we scan the queues. My husband points to the "singles queue"— it moves a lot faster. He jumps to the next gondola, and I take the one that follows. There are five Indian gentlemen in the cabin. Not long after the lift starts climbing, they introduce themselves and their elderly companion.

"He is our village chief. He does not touch women, look at them, or speak to them." The village elder wears a pagri, and he is dressed in very down-to-earth colors. He stares fixedly out the window. In a way, I feel sorry to have bothered them with my presence, as he cannot now freely communicate with his companions. The men, on the other hand, are very interested in a young snowboarder woman traveling seemingly on her own.

Engelberg in Switzerland is famous for its glaciers, so there are always visitors from all around the world. Most tourists take the lift to the glacier and photograph themselves, walk around a bit, and take the lift down again. They are often dressed in their national wardrobes—nothing that would keep them warm in such altitude. After working for a Swiss company, I grew fond of the Swiss Alps, so we have kept coming here and the slopes near Chamonix and Zermatt.

"Are you traveling alone?" one of the men asked.

"No, my husband just took the prior lift; this is a faster way for us than queueing to go together," I replied.

They seem to accept that as a respectable answer and continue their curious questions. "I suppose you have the luxury of using your husband's credit card and enjoying the holiday here," one of the men said.

I get that a lot from some cultures, so I just keep smiling and explaining how things in the Nordics work. I tell them about my job and travels and that I pay my way, including any shopping that I do. This baffles them greatly.

"Do you have children?" one of the men asked.

This is a question that is bound to come up. I tell them that I do not have children, nor do I plan to have any. Now, their faces are confused, and a few of them laugh.

"Why? In our country, you would be divorced in no time. We all have families. We could not imagine a life without children," one of the men said.

I expected this response, so I just kept smiling and said, "I am very happy for you. It is wonderful to have a family. I, however, am not afraid of getting divorced, as I own my house, and I have plenty of savings to sustain me while I work." As I watch, their faces change—they realize that I am a different kind of woman than they ever imagined.

"Wow!" one of them said aloud. "Imagine that! I think I like Western women. You cover your shopping, your credit cards; you work, own a house. We pay for everything for our family. Marrying here does not sound bad at all."

At the top station, I climb out of the lift, wish them a good journey, and grab my snowboard. I see women wearing colorful saris at the plateau, their jewelry and décor reflecting the sun like golden sparkles. I am happy that our worlds met. This is what I like about traveling; the winding cultural paths coming together in a distant mountain. We come from completely different backgrounds, yet these men were far more polite than many I had met in my culture.

Remember: Even if we are different, we can learn to find richness in diversity. I have been a role model to women who have known me. They always expected me to succeed. I knew my strength was limited. In Finland, women cannot stay at home. They need to work the same as men to sustain sufficient income. I could do either or—not both. So, I chose *security*. Yes, you must consider what you value the most. Each life is unique. I chose security over children. Not just my own, but my family's. My parents could not finance our future. I could not change that past. But I could be there for my sisters. I could change the future, even if just a little. Given the choice, I would still choose this path of love—and that meant choosing well for a career.

The Fairy Princess

Butterfly's wings carry a tale—sensitive and daring. It is a story of survival carried by a butterfly's flight over restless seas and windy meadows—as if fueled by the light of the sun. A small life that wanders like a great adventurer. —Maria Lehtman, dedicated to Sophia (2014)

The year 2001

It is cold and dark like January in the North always is. The days are still short, and sunlight is scarce. The past months have been like a black fog in my mind. Both my older sister and my mother have been widowed. In the middle of all this, there is a spark of light. My youngest sister has been struggling immensely with her first pregnancy. She has had to spend time in the hospital to secure her pregnancy. Every day counts. With still several weeks to go until the optimal date, the baby is born. I am on my way to see her. When I step into the hospital room, I see the tiniest girl I have ever set my eyes on. She looks like a little fairy princess. Her fingers are smaller than matchsticks. My sister is already used to holding her. I cannot imagine how. The baby only weighs about 1.6 kg (3.5 pounds).

I sit down on a chair, and the nurse, my friend's mother, hands me a pillow. Gently, the little fairy princess is lowered to the pillow, leaning against my arm. I am afraid she will slip away underneath my arm. Her entire body could be held in my hands. She is only four days old. I feel blessed to be her auntie. At that moment, a bond emerges that never breaks again. I cannot define a word for this type of love that is mixed with admiration and protectiveness—like the earth would look after the moon. Each in their place, time, and course, yet bound by the celestial bonds.

The little fairy princess wins over hearts wherever she goes. Like her mother when she was a child, my fairy princess has blond, curly hair and big blue eyes, and she loves to perform. She dances whenever she hears music and even when there is none. She is the most adorable child to spend time with. She loves drawing, music, and watching animated movies. When she gets hurt, I cry. When she is happy, I feel joy. Not a day goes by that I do not think of her or feel an echo of her emotions.

Remember: Being different does not mean that you are not fulfilling your purpose. Be the purpose. Answer the call. Trust your intuition. Children, as we previously learned, consider that as an adult, you already see the truth. If you feel someone needs you, it is most likely because they do. There is no greater purpose than sharing unconditional love.

The Conflict

I stand on a precipice
There is as much distance to the sky
As there is to the bottom of the abyss
One needs to just lean in quietly
Reaching out to the clouds
And fall with the loose stones and pebbles
And then -
The sky opens
—Maria Lehtman (1995)

The year 2006

I am 34 years old and on extended sick leave from work, preparing to move to another position. My physiotherapist calls my back "the armor." She uses acupuncture, and the pins are barely through my skin. My nerves are so agitated that everything hurts. The muscles in my back are like the strings of a violin sprung too tight.

I come home one day a few weeks after my sick leave has started. It is August—right after our 10th anniversary. My husband wants to discuss children. I rear up like a lioness. He is upset and says that I am being impossible if I do not even engage in a discussion. Finally, I calmed down.

"You assured me that you did not want children. I asked you many times before we got married to ensure that you understood," I remark.

"Yes, but that was then. This is now," he says. "Things can change. Perhaps I want children, after all."

A stunned silence. I am at the edge of my capacity to handle any more stress. And yet, there is nothing I can do. I know he is right. How could he have known all those years ago what it would mean to him in the future? All his siblings are married and have children, all five of them. We are the only ones to have broken the pattern. He is also against adoption, so we never discuss options, and in all honesty, that would not make things any easier for me. For most of these 10 years, I have taken care of our finances so that he could build a business. There was no room for a child in my life. I did not make it to the United Nations; I chose the IT industry, international, busy, demanding, challenging, and a rare choice for a woman in my circles.

We continue to discuss, and finally, my husband picks up some of his things and leaves. He does not say for how long. I sit in our bedroom and cry. There is nothing I can do. I love him, but this decision is for him to make.

After a few days, we agreed to have a date in a café downtown. We sat outside in the chill late August breeze, looking at the sea. We talked just like in good old times. Finally, it was time to leave, so I asked him where he wanted to go.

"Home," he said. "I have not yet made up my mind, but I would like to be home all the same."

And so began my journey into the unknown. For the first time in our marriage, I was not certain that love was enough.

You could say that communication is the best way to untangle differences. However, sometimes, love requires that you accept reality as it is. I had no intention of convincing my husband to think differently, just as he knew that trying to talk me into having children was pointless. We were at a stalemate.

I was fortunate to find a new job quickly and move on in my life otherwise. I established a company. One of the first digital enterprises that I could easily run from home. The income was mainly additional funding that financed my equipment and licenses for photography.

However, this indecision of my loved one was constantly at the back of my mind. I rarely visit therapists and usually only consult them on a specific situation. After a few months, I was so distraught that I went to see one—I just surfed the internet and selected a therapist by intuition. I wanted a male psychologist specifically. Someone who would be able to see the other side of the situation. It was the second-best decision I had made during that half a year; the first one was leaving a job that lately had just consumed me.

I sat with unease on the chair at the therapist's office and explained my situation. I told him that I loved my husband, and I did not want to divorce him.

He looked at me and said, "Why? You do not have to divorce him. He is the uncertain one who needs to decide. You are right to love him and wish to continue forward with your marriage. Nothing in this situation forces you to act."

In that instant, my eyes opened. The core me was always the problem-solver; the person who took action to correct matters, resolve issues, and act. So, I instinctively thought I would need to start a process for separation. I leaned back in the chair and felt a great weight lift from my shoulders. All I could do now was to love and hope.

To help my healing, I booked a vacation trip alone to Southern Italy and sealed my passion with Italy, especially the region of Calabria. I rented a car and drove to the mountains and beach sides with a few female companions who came on the same flight from Finland. It was the first vacation trip I had made alone during our marriage. Of course, for work, I extended my trips here and there to photograph and see the sites, but I never went on a vacation trip. It was empowering, and yet, every time I saw something special, I thought, *He would love this view as well.* That is how close we were. No experience was quite complete without the other.

Remember: The evolution of relationships will always happen, whether you have children or not. Nothing is guaranteed. Emotional growth has its challenges. We can never tell what the future brings, but do not let go of love. Sometimes you need to love yourself more than the partnership, and at times your love for it saves it. Look for help and support. Objective wisdom is never wasted.

The Prayer

You cannot measure the feeling of love
It can be grand
Limitless
Powerful enough to reach the sky
Or invisible joy
At the bottom of your stomach
Like a fairy's dance
On a rose petal
Unconditional desire
To give a hug
An expression through
A play of words
Or a glimmer of the eye

Love forms
A timeless memory
We can return to
Over and over again
—Maria Lehtman, dedicated to our mother (2016)

The Year 2008

We sit around the kitchen table at one of our relatives' home. Many of my husband's siblings are there with their children. At the end of the celebration, we take pictures, and then one of them talks about prayers.

Finally looking at me, the person says, "I pray for you too. I keep praying that you will finally have children."

I am utterly speechless. By then, we had long since forgotten our difficulties about the subject with my husband. My career has taken good turns, and I feel that I am finally in a corporate culture where I fit in. My health is challenging, but I can manage. I am one of the few flagged in an international talent program, so my dream of gaining a leadership position is closer than ever. There are so many children in our families that at Christmas time, I typically just wish for noise-cancelling headphones. They are all sweet, beautiful, and talented—but as I do not come from a big family, I feel that I need more peace. I watch my husband play with them and enjoy the fun and games. I could not imagine him in any other way. While he plays, I sometimes draw coloring pictures for the children. They like princesses and horses. I enjoy the joyful glimmer in their eyes when they receive a new drawing.

I always pray for the universe to give my loved ones light, love, and support. Nothing more, nothing less. We cannot know what the other person wants or needs. We do not know their purpose in life, their mission, their journey, or the adversities they go through. With love, we can gain a wider perspective—but it requires patience.

Remember: You are a vessel, not the solution. The universe will work out what is best for everyone. Support each other. Love does not give all the answers. It follows along different paths and destinies that all lead to great light and self-awareness.

My Fairy Godson

Love life
like the shooting stars
In the winter sky
Moments filled with love
Light and kindness
Soulful memories
That light up the sky
And the heart
—Maria Lehtman, 2019

The Year 2014

I am sitting on our terrace with my younger sister. She has exciting news to share with me. My sister is six years younger than me. There are four girls in our family. As our mother had several miscarriages, I have always thought our brothers decided to stay as our guardians in the stars.

"I am pregnant," my sister says with anticipation, joy, and dismay all mixed up. She is frightened. She has always feared labor. For a good reason, women in our family all had difficulties during pregnancy and labor. When I was born, I spent my first three weeks isolated in an oxygen cabinet.

I hugged my sister and felt happy for her. When she left, I broke down. I was the last one, the last of the sisters in my family and my husband's not to have children. It felt easier when I had someone on my side. An ally. A woman who understood how it all looks to an outsider. I feel more alone now than ever. I feel guilty for my sorrow. But I know how women change when they become mothers. It always makes me feel that I have become a second-class citizen in their lives. That my love for their children is not credible unless I have children of my own. Depression takes over me my entire emotion spectrum becomes distorted.

My sister asks if I would like to be her child's fairy godmother—neither of them belongs to the church, which is quite normal in Finland. Being a

Christian means additional taxes that only a few want to pay for visiting the church four times in their lives: the christening, the confirmation, the wedding, and the funeral.

I am delighted to be the fairy godparent—I share the position with her husband's brother. Their child, after all, will be the first on his side. Not soon after, I find out that they are expecting a boy. I keep my secret with me. No one likes spoilers. He is full of energy, and very soon, his spirit teachers begin to approach me from time to time. I want to help the child, but my heart is constantly conflicted. This is a paradigm shift in my life. I need to embrace the fact that I will be questioned and criticized and receive smirky remarks whenever I am around children. That is how mothers are. I understand it. I also know that as each sister becomes a mother, I only have a fraction of their time. The bond between us never disappears, but the relationship is forever changed.

Three months later, I had that moment in the hotel room with my fairy godson and my broken heart. I do not feel sorry for not having children; I feel saddened that I am different. My only solace comes from my mother who says that my grandmother was the same way. She had said aloud that she cared not for having children. She loved them. She took good care of them. However, she would rather have led a life without being a mother. One can hardly blame her. She lived a lonely mother's life through three major wars with a husband who fought in all three. Her position was radically different from mine. Still, it made me think that perhaps there was something in our genealogy that brought on this mindset.

In the coming months, my fairy godson's teachers would approach me more and more frequently, and I got used to his presence. We practiced a lot. He was like a rainbow child, not by the New Age definition but someone with honed skills to be agile in the physical and metaphysical world. A child with a wide aura. What had taken me months to learn, he became proficient in hours. I taught him how to build shields, how to fight with light energy, how to create and manage mini galaxies, how to navigate dreams, how to practice energy healing, and the list goes on. Hours and hours of lessons.

A miracle happened. Every time we met, my carefully woven shields became a tiny bit thinner. In the end, just before he was born, I suddenly realized that I had no regret in me, no guilt, no sorrow, no shame, or depression. Instead, all I had was love and light. I was looking forward to meeting my little godson from the stars. The spirit teachers knew that my heart had been broken—to be whole again, I needed to love and have children to love. They never had to be my own—and I did not have to let go of my sisters altogether.

My fairy godson had an arduous entry into the world. It nearly cost their lives. I am grateful that my sister and her son made it through. What surprised everyone was that as a baby, my fairy godson never shied away from me. Even when I lived abroad, and we had not seen each other for months, he immediately came into my arms and felt I was his kin. Everyone thought it must have been because my sister and I have very similar voices. The little prince and I knew the truth. Our bond was cosmic.

Whenever I was ill, our little prince popped into my lucid dreams. He would check up on me and leave as soon as I said in my mind that everything was all right. Even when I nearly died of pneumonia, he told his mother that everything was all right. I just needed someone to play with. Right, he was. I did not intend to go. I had a family. Ohana.

Remember: You are worthy. You are loved. Your love is priceless. Let love heal you. The universe will always try to find a way to help you if you let it. Family can be anything you want it to be. Time with the elderly; volunteering to take care of children; adopting furbabies; being an aunt or an uncle; being a sponsor, a teacher, or a mentor—there are so many ways in the world today to find a purpose. And many souls waiting for someone to find them.

The Fairy Godson's Lesson
The Year 2016

Ta-dah!" exclaimed our two-year-old little Houdini, and the gift for our mother's 74th birthday, a beautiful violet pansy brooch, vanished from sight. Fortunately, the brooch was still there, safe and sound. My fairy godson, however, was more interested in the box and the mystery surrounding how the gift appeared inside it. It got me thinking about the secrets of life and where the wonderful things around us come from. We often overlook the fact that the very framework of life is a mystery in itself. The moving beings and things that surround us are like boxes waiting to be explored with childlike imagination and curiosity. Even a simple sandbox can ignite a sense of wonder and questions like "How was it created?" and "How can I use it?" Note to myself: Always retain a childlike curiosity and imagination and never stop exploring the mysteries of life.

The Year 2023

More children are entering our lives. Two little princesses were born to my older sister's sons. I am a great-auntie now, and I am proud of it. Two of my kin have decided not to have children. I respect their choices, and I would never question them about their decision. I have not asked why. That is my nature. Unless someone wishes to share with me, I do not feel it is my place to ask. After all, I know how hard the topic was for me. And I can see they, like me, still want to be part of the world of children.

Love has a much wider and deeper spectrum than we can ever fathom. Imagine a being, older than time, filled with light, an eternal mother. Someone like Mother Earth who has lived for eons and learned to love all beings as her own. Are they hers? Did they come from another lineage? Does it matter? No. Only love matters—infinite, patient, unconditional, and forgiving.

The Now

Love is ageless,
Timeless
And filled with hope
It stretches beyond our comprehension
It has no rules

But in true light
It walks with grace
Keep your love in light
Let it shine
With patience and care
—Maria Lehtman (2023)

I want to thank all the wonderful children who have allowed me to be an auntie in their lives. I cherish my role. I did not peek through all the windows in the past to write my story. Nor did I write about all the children in my life. I wrote as my intuition guided me. Í want you to know that I have no regrets. I have valuable relationships that will ensure love stays in my life. I have traveled. I have struggled. I have learned. I have created a wonderful career I can be proud of. I have manifested my dreams—all of them and more. The 20-year-old me had foresight. I am grateful that she stayed true to herself.

Remember: Love yourself. Love is all.

About Maria Lehtman

 Maria Lehtman is a passionate author who resides in Finland, in the beautiful Nordic region. With over 20 years of experience in sales, marketing, and professional services, she has made a career in telecommunications. She has achieved many accomplishments throughout her employment, including leading successful global Transition, Transformation, and Competency programs. Currently, Maria works in the International Marketing department, focusing on developing transversal employee and executive social media engagement programs.

Maria is an advocate for digital empowerment and the opportunities it provides for people worldwide. She is also a devoted photographer and digital artist frequently engaged in creative projects. As a compassionate leader, Maria's mission is to support individuals in self-transformation and embracing new skills. Her trademark is her ability to share a smile even during the most challenging circumstances while maintaining a "mindfulness" attitude.

Maria is a featured contributor and columnist at the award-winning new media agency BizCatalyst 360˚. Her posts and thoughts represent her view of the world. She is a contributing author to four motivational anthologies; her latest story is part of the Amazon bestselling Mission Hope series, *Volume II, Inspirational Stories of Faith and Triumph with Char Murphy and the Motivation Champs Media*. Additionally, she has published two poetic photography journey books, *Dew Drops* and *The Dreaming Doors - Through the Soul Gateways*. Her writing is focused on sharing beauty, inspiration, love, and hope with others.

For your information:

Author page on Amazon:

	www.amazon.com/author/marialehtman
Amazon:	Maria's publications:
	Hiljainen Hetki (Dew Drops) and The Dreaming Doors
Amazon:	Motivation Champs Media collaboration with Char Murphy: Mission Hope, Thriving Through Seasons of the Soul and Amazon Bestseller (Transformation): Mission Hope Volume 2, Inspirational Stories of Faith and Triumph
Amazon:	Sacred Stories collaboration: Chaos to Clarity: Sacred Stories of Transformational Change and Crappy to Happy: Sacred Stories of Transformational Joy
Columnist:	www.bizcatalyst360.com/author/marialehtman
Website:	thedigitalteacup.com
Instagram:	@thedigitalteacup and @marialehtman
Twitter:	@LehtmanMaria
LinkedIn:	linkedin.com/in/marialehtman

Living with Slim Hope

—

Ali Anani, Ph.D.

Let me start by sharing my late father's story. I am sure that if you read it, you will find a rich life story filled with hope, even though hope appeared to be very slim.

I was about 10 years old when my father had an ulcer with a bleeding stomach. The doctor told him that he had two more years to live, and if he operated on him, the chances of my father's survival would not exceed 2%.

My father replied by saying that he wanted to have the surgery in a year's time. He wanted to secure his family financially before having the life-threatening surgery. His chances of living would then not exceed 1%, his doctor advised him.

My father was operated on for more than four hours and had 50% of his stomach removed. He survived. Unfortunately, my father had a cold with severe coughing. The surgery threads went loose; the wound opened, and the naked eye could see my father's stomach.

The surgeon was at a loss what to do. He told my father that he had to operate him again but without anesthetics. This was because his body would not have tolerated anesthetics. My father told him that there was no problem. His faith in God was so rooted that he believed it was only God's will to test his endurance and faith. Imagine that the surgeon did the surgery without my father complaining of pain. He lived for more than thirty years post-surgery.

One Year of Hard Work

My father spent the year before his surgery was due in working on several jobs. He gave English private lessons, newscaster, and translator, prepared bids for a major construction company, and many more.

While working for the construction company, he knew of their lost case of a project. The client failed to pay the last payment approximating an equivalent of 75 English pounds. My father expressed his willingness to reopen the case. The company agreed on one condition—that he would do it on his time, and not the company's working hours. My father agreed.

He contacted a famous English lawyer who agreed to work on the case. Six months of exchanging information mostly by phone and dispatch of documents passed. Finally, the lawyer won the case.

The company celebrated the great "victory." When my father asked for his reward, the company told him, "There is no money for you. You should have asked for an agreeable fee, but you did not." My father got furious. The company finally agreed to pay him 500 pounds. When my father received the due amount the next morning, it was only 400 pounds. The company gave 100 pounds to the helping staff. My father resigned immediately. The company accepted his resignation only after he had completed a bid he had been working on lately. My father finished the bid and left.

A few days later, a man knocked on our door. He mentioned that he required a meeting with my father urgently. The man offered my father 15,000 pounds if he would disclose the final amount of the bid he prepared for his old company. The man owned a competing contracting company. The man told my father that it was time to get revenge on his old company. My father replied by saying that it was not his way to correct a mistake by making a bigger one. He terminated the meeting immediately.

The offer of 15,000 pounds at that time was enough to sustain our family for 10 years, at least. Despite this temptation, my father stood firm in his beliefs and principles. What made him so ethical and a man of values? Please continue reading to find the answer.

The Triangle of Living a Sustainable Life

The triangle of living a sustainable life is similar to the triangle of fire. To have a fire, we need a source of heat to ignite the fuel consisting of a burning material and oxygen—without which, there shall be no fire. What is the equivalent of the triangle of sustainable life? These are faith, hope, and love.

Faith is the source of ignition. It is the source of heat. Hope is the oxygen that makes living possible. Love is the fuel that keeps life propagating. Take the story of my father, for example, and apply the triangle of living a sustainable life to understand it. My father needed faith to undergo surgery, despite there being a mere 1% probability of it being life-saving. Hope was the oxygen that burnt his desire to survive and accept the big challenge. It was the realization that if one door closes, another door will open. It was the belief that no matter how dark the sky is, a bright dawn will follow.

It was the conviction that wearing the eyeglasses of hope, no matter how slim hope is, soon it would expand. Love sustained my father's belief that life was going to be rosy after all. Love helped my father to be hopeful that things would turn out better. My father believed that having faith, hope, and love would generate a synergistic effect that would nourish his life. There would be no triangle of sustainable life if one of the three components is missing. When all of them are present, miracles happen.

I lived my father's story, which taught me the same lessons. I am sharing them with you, hoping that by sharing our stories, we may lead better lives.

About Ali Anani

 Ali Anani got his doctorate in chemistry from the UK in 1973. After a successful career in research and teaching at universities, his interest suddenly shifted to studying complex human behavior using his scientific background to help him find new thinking paths and novel ideas.

His interest resulted in writing more than eight e-books and two novels in Arabic and more than 1,000 articles and presentations.

He wrote several articles and presentations using visual metaphors in story writing. One of his presentations enjoyed more than 30,000 views. His research on human paradoxes and biases helped him develop new approaches to his writing.

Ugly Shoes and Love

MaLinda Jo Perry

I guess I never really thought much about the power of love, growing up. It wasn't until later in life I learned the power of love comes to us in every little thing or experience. It's in those daily glimmers, those moments in time that make us smile or take our breath away for just a moment in time. Then before we realize it, a million glimmers turn into those bigger moments where we learn our biggest lessons and make the ultimate impact on ourselves and those around us.

I was born knocked kneed, bow-legged, club-footed, and pigeon-toed (say that three times fast). The chances of me walking normally were slim until the Shriners stepped in. My parents didn't have the money or opportunity for surgery, so they opted for the next best thing. A full leg cast on each leg, with a stabilizing bar between my legs, then Forest Gump leg braces for several years; next in the lineup was the most hideous pair of corrective shoes. This was an open opportunity and invitation for bullying. Me and my ugly shoes became open season for insults and teasing. My grandma, Dorothy, would paint my ugly shoes every Sunday night to match my dresses for the week. She would tell me all the time, "Just smile, pretty, and be sweet, and no one will notice your shoes."

As my feet and legs got better, I graduated to wearing these extremely uncomfortable inserts in my shoes that were made of fiberglass. Comfort was never an option, and neither were pretty sandals. Nope, I wore lace-up saddle oxfords designed to look like they were being worn on the wrong feet. This usually involved nasty comments from peers that cut clear to the soul. Let me tell you; those shoes showed me quickly who my friends were going to be. Because of Dorothy's power of love, I believed I had the most beautiful shoes because she loved me enough to paint them. Every Sunday night, after dinner, we would pick out all my dresses for the week, and she would set my shoes on the kitchen table and start painting them. She would paint the white part of the saddle shoes. Some weeks, I had blue shoes; some weeks, red ones. The absolute best was when she would paint them pink! What little girl wouldn't love to have pink shoes?

I was the only one in my class to talk about a happy heart! I remember so badly wanting to wear some plain white Keds tennis shoes to a Fourth of July party, and my bonus mom said absolutely not until I had worn my corrective shoes for 8 hours … Ugh! That power of love also gave me the courage to fly. I took dance and cheerleading with the hopes of building stronger leg muscles and straightening out my legs and feet. I even became the double Dutch jump rope champion in fourth grade because I had these amazing, magical-painted shoes. Living in Texas where cheerleading starts at a very early age became my godsend because saddle shoes were just part of the uniform, and I immediately fit in without even trying. Before long, I was a top cheerleader with a three-foot vertical jump! Resilience, persistence, and patience became the name of the game, and none would have been achieved without Dorothy's power of love and one hideous pair of shoes.

I met Shari in kindergarten because of those ugly shoes. She was the only one brave enough to ask me about them. We became fast friends, and she never cared about my shoes. We were inseparable and spent every waking moment we could together. Living two blocks away from her house allowed me to be part of a big family. She had two sisters and a little brother. It was loud and fun, with plenty to do. One of my greatest joys was going to Shari's house and shedding the shoes. Going barefoot was a common adventure at her house. My house became Shari's refuge where she could be like an only child. We used to say all the time, "Wouldn't it be great if we were sisters?" As little girls, becoming sisters was our biggest dream next to being famous like the Carpenters! Then, one magical encounter; well, I like to think it was magical, but it was actually a case of unknown identity when her dad met my mom. He was doing some work at her office building and recognized her name when he asked her if I would be going with him to New Mexico. She had no idea who he was, and she said to him, "I don't know who the hell you are, but my daughter isn't going anywhere with you!" In all those years of friendship between Shari and me, they never knew each other because he was serving in Vietnam. Exactly 10 days after their first meeting, they were married, and my best friend became my sister! Our childhood dream came true! I remember asking my mom once how they could get married so fast after only knowing each other for ten days. She said, «When you know, you know.» Love is that powerful. It's amazing how the power of love can move from one event like ugly shoes to another and carry with it even more amazing lessons. Those ugly shoes gave me a sister! My very best friend became my sister! Those hideous, painful, ugly shoes brought me the big family I always wanted!

With a new blended family, the power of love taught us the lessons of teamwork, togetherness, and compassion. There were no books, no self-help groups, and blended families were rare indeed. We had the Brady Bunch to guide us, and trust me, our lives were nothing like the TV show. My parents did this amazing thing on our first night as a family; they held a family meeting. What? Not one family I knew ever had a family meeting. This is where they set clear boundaries and some pretty strict rules about being a team forever. I have no doubt this came from my dad's military background; once a captain, always a captain. My dad's idea of adventure and family time had us loading up in the ‹70s' purple van with a psychedelic paint job and shag carpet. We would load up early on a Saturday morning with a cooler packed full of sandwiches, chips, and pop and hit the Wyoming backroads for some old west landmark, fish hatchery, or cemetery.

This new family and new life brought with it so many blessings. Being a child of two blended families gave me grandparents! Lots and lots of grandparents! At one point, I had 12 living grands and great-grands! I don't know many children who can honestly say that. These were more than just new members of an extended family; they WERE my family. My heart was full of love and gratitude. Those ugly shoes gave me the presence of grit and resilience. I would say those qualities are a gift. My mom would tell you that they were a handful. I didn't know how to hold back. I was this bossy little girl who came into their lives with passion and gusto. I gave them no other choice but to be my family. So many of our family events had four generations in attendance. The wonderful, most beautiful lessons came with each event. Lessons of life, love, and history. I know what you are thinking, "How is this possible? And so many people? There must be drama.» Nope, no drama. Every person in this extended family believed we put our differences aside for the benefit of the kids. Not once did I ever think of my bonus mom or bonus dad's parents as anything other than my grandparents, and they treated me exactly as if I was born into their family. There were even times when my real dad, both sets of his parents (blended family), bonus mom and her parents, my mom, bonus dad, step-sister, and half-siblings all went on vacation together. No, this is not normal by most family standards, but I'm proof that it is possible, and it makes for an amazing life. When you think about the lessons we learn while growing up—you know, how to be kind and grateful—and then add four generations among several different walks of life, those lessons come three-fold. I would say these lessons were the beginning of finding a way to pay it forward, but sadly, no. I had so many more lessons to endure before I would be able to pay it forward.

In an ideal world, the bullying would have ended when I started wearing normal shoes. That would be way too easy. The gifts of grit and resilience became stronger with each new phase of life. In fifth grade, a miracle happened!! I was finally allowed to wear normal shoes. I can't even begin to tell you how excited I was. My mom took me to a Buster Brown shoe store. Back in the day, this was considered an expensive store. I remember I couldn't contain my excitement. When we arrived, I was overwhelmed by all the styles and choices. It was literally this little girl's dream. Then within all the excitement came a burst of defeat. All the beautiful shoes I dreamed of wearing came to a screeching halt. There was only one pair of shoes that would house the fiberglass inserts I would be wearing. That's it! Just one pair! They're oxfords!!! Dreams crushed instantly. These oxfords were different. Yes, they were white, but the side panels were this navy plaid with little green and gold lines running through it. They were really different. This was a new lesson bestowed on me by my mother. She said, "Style is not what you wear but how you wear it, and no one else will have shoes like yours." She taught me that style is what you make it, and it's OK to be unique. For a very brief moment, I wanted the ugly painted shoe back. I wanted the comfort of what was because I already knew how to answer that. I had owned it for so many years. Was I really ready to show up now with a new style? I guess I was … So, on that day in the Buster Brown shoe store, my painted ugly shoes pushed me forward again out of my comfort zone and into a new reality. A reality full of embracing my new style with confidence. A confidence I have never known before. One where I was present in my own skin and not hiding behind the ugly shoes. This newfound presence given to me by Dorothy's partnership with the ugly painted shoes gave me confidence. After all, I didn't need the shoes to show me what my next move was going to be. It was my opportunity to shine and move through life in new shoes. The funny thing is, I still have a fondness for blue plaids. Who knew?

A move from west Texas to the wild west of Wyoming brought new adventures in the wild West. New kid in a new state, new school, new grade, and new culture. I had this fearless Scarlett O'Hara attitude that life was going to be great! No more ugly shoes to hold me back and keep me grounded. *Au contraire, mon ami!* I quickly learned that there are a lot of mean people in this world, and they begin showing their colors at 11 years of age. I was the "new girl" from a place none of these girls have ever visited. I had the short, sassy Dorothy Hamill haircut; spoke with a funny accent; and somehow thought I could just smile pretty and fit right in. The local girls did not share this belief. In walks decade number two of bullying. I spent the first four months crying by myself and being angry at my parents for wanting to give me a better life filled with opportunities. "Just be sweet and smile pretty" rang through those tears every single day. Eventually, Dorothy's anthem rang true. Those mean girls did finally come around to accepting me. I asked my mom once how it was; I never became a mean girl since most of the girls I knew were. She very matter-of-factly said, "Your positivity would never allow it."

The next few decades brought a new anthem to light. This one came from my mom. I found that mean people are literally everywhere! So many unhappy people sharing unhappy comments and speaking angry, condescending truths. Everywhere you turn, someone is trying their best to just exist, and the intention of their unhappiness is projected onto others. My mom taught me to just "consider the source." This is a very deep and powerful lesson for a 13-year-old. Consider. The. Source. What does that mean really? Every time I ran into someone who felt the need to boldly tell me what they didn't like about me or chose to find a new way to bully me, my mom would say, "Consider the source." This mantra stuck with me for years. If you were to ask my mom what this actually means, she would say, "Is their opinion really fact? Do you hold value in their beliefs?" The answer is always no! No, no, no! Their opinion of who I am is not my worth. Do I want to be like these people in any way? No. Is there value in their opinions or words? No. My ugly shoes taught me that surface items, pretty or ugly, are not who we are. Positivity, kindness, grace, gratitude … these are what we are and what we bring to the table. Ugly shoes just give us opportunities for lessons. Sort of like speed bumps in life. Slowly and cautiously moving us forward to something better. Those speed bumps allow us to be aware of our surroundings before the next big adventure. When I became a Gallup Strengths coach, I learned that gratitude, happiness, and positivity are virtues we are not born with; they must be taught. I believe with all my heart that my deformed feet, my ugly painted shoes, my grandma Dorothy, and the strength and grit of a single mom who would never allow me to feel sorry for myself taught me the virtues of gratitude, happiness, and positivity. Those ugly painted shoes and every single person who bullied me taught me the power of love. This love gave me grit, resilience, gratitude, and the ability to share my voice with others.

This power allows each of us to be the difference between meanness and light. I chose to become a teacher and a voice for all those who never had a Grandma Dorothy or a mom to say, "Consider the source." So many times, over the last several years, I have found myself saying to someone who has been beaten and broken by the meanness of others that it's not about you. You are kind; you are beautiful; you have amazing gifts that you bring to the table. It's about the other person because happy girls don't do that. When I started the nonprofit Happy Girls Don't Do That, its main goal was to educate youth on gratitude, happiness, and positivity through individual development, community development, and social global influencing development. I soon realized that yes, the littles need these lessons. They need to build strength, grit, and resilience through the power of positivity and kindness, starting with gratitude. However, I learned very quickly that everyone can benefit from these lessons. I learned there are a lot of broken people in this world who need to understand that they are not ugly shoes. I have realized it is a mission to ignite a global movement where individuals of all ages and backgrounds are empowered and inspired to lead lives overflowing with gratitude, happiness, love, and unwavering positivity. I envision a world where the darkness of negativity is replaced by the radiant light of hope, resilience, and boundless strength.

The power of those ugly painted shoes was meant to be shared. It's a gift to those who feel the only thing everyone sees is ugly shoes. It's the power of being unapologetically authentic. Once we see the ugly shoes as an opportunity to shine what is brightest within us, then the power of love can be shared.

About MaLinda Jo Perry

Embark on the inspiring journey of MaLinda Jo Perry, a Wyoming-raised and global adventurer, whose life weaves a tapestry of diverse experiences. From the heart of Wyoming to the whirlwind of international travels, MaLinda's story unfolds as a captivating narrative of a hockey mom turned successful entrepreneur.

As the driving force behind MaLinda Perry Consulting, LLC, MaLinda brings over 25 years of expertise in business, non-profit, education, and leadership. Her transformative approach, rooted in strengths-based coaching, workshops, and leadership development, has earned her recognition as a Gallup Certified Strengths coach and an Incredible Family Master coach.

A dynamic speaker and action-oriented coach, MaLinda thrives at the intersection of inspiration and action. Her commitment to fueling success in a diverse environment, coupled with her role as the executive director and founder of Happy Girls Don't Do That, reflects a deep dedication to holistic development and organizational growth.

MaLinda's journey as a leadership consultant showcases her ability to consult with leaders at all levels, fostering employee and customer engagement and implementing strategic initiatives for business growth. This is a guide to personal and leadership development, where she empowers individuals to identify and maximize their unique talents.

Through Gallup's Strengths Finder, MaLinda Perry Consulting, LLC, helps readers discover their innate talents and transform them into strengths for personal and professional effectiveness. MaLinda's top five strengths—Strategic, Adaptability, Achiever, Positivity, and Ideation—serve as a testament to her well-rounded qualities and expertise in guiding others toward their best selves.

Vampires of Love

———

Rebecca Blondie Amelia

How long does it take before you do not feel completely depleted after someone has sucked the life out of you? You do not realize the depths of depletion—just how empty, on every level, one can feel—until sometimes very long after you are out of the situation. Sometimes, suddenly, you have waves of realization where you are lacking what was taken by the "vampire." I was overwhelmed with that feeling this morning. I have doubted if I will ever have the capacity to find the empath in me, the source where love freely flowed from me before I was "choked." I have learned that certain personalities were developed to take love from others when one has not learned to find their own inner love source, or they lack empathy and know it, so they fake it by imitating (stealing) yours and then criticizing you for something or another to create chaos. I mistook the "love bombing" as authentic love. Once I felt safe inside that relationship, I freely gave everything I had. And love was at the source of everything I gave. My finances, my emotions, and my empathy freely ran like a never-ending river. I joyfully gave all I had. I gave it to a "love vampire." I had no idea until 18 years later when I woke up one day and realized there was a mountain of chaos inside and all around me.

I started to notice that I felt increasingly and at times literally "choked." I felt emotions, pure joy, love, fun, playfulness, and words I wanted to express get stuck and crammed in my throat, as I was stopped from being able to let them loose. I started to notice less and less "love" flowing toward me and more flowing from me. And then it began to freeze like a river inside of me with the icy winds blowing back at me. WHAT? I was lost. Little by little, various forms of mistreatment began. At the time, I did not recognize it for what it was. I was too busy looking inward and finding new ways not to feel squelched every day. I was too busy trying to help the other party discover what I already knew and trying to figure out what it would take for the other person to break into those levels so badly missing. What affected me most deeply was my disconnect from my deep intuition and empathy. I was involved with not only a "love vampire" but an "intuition scrambler." And this is love?

For me, deep levels of love are reserved for a core group and come from a different source than the love I feel when I am so happy meeting new people, seeing a new baby or kids playing, or greeting a friend in town; just the everyday love I felt exuding from every pore of my body. I was constantly being told, "I will find deep levels of love with or without you." This is within a committed relationship. I looked inward for what I could do to help that person. I had no idea the treadmill I was running on had a speed and intensity that continued to increase until the day I was knocked off that treadmill, bagged up like trash, and left at the curb. Yes, just like that and just as cruel. But that is a different story and one I touched upon in my chapter on "Healing Generational Pain" in the second of this Mission Hope series. Love is such a broad topic; I did not know where to begin.

So, this morning, as I sat here, with total writer's block and a two-day deadline, I responded to a friend's text about her need to get things done today. I suggested, to avoid feeling overwhelmed, that she write each task on a sticky notepad, leave the pages on the pad, and—as she completes each task—pull it off the pad and put it on the bathroom mirror so she could see what she accomplished. It focuses on one task at a time. Suddenly, it occurred to me that this could translate to writing. That is how I finally broke my "writer's block"! I am hoping I can use this same method to simplify a path to opening myself up again. Opening to giving and receiving love as freely as I did before, not only to my "core group," but this time, with less naiveté, a better understanding, and less desire to be on constant guard with people I do not know. I have contributed to that which keeps channels blocked. I have an understanding of how I am where I am. Where I have been stuck is how to take steps to move forward. For me, it begins with narrowing the focus; like the sticky pad, write it down. The first word that came to mind was a resounding "VAMPIRE!"

After dealing with a "love vampire" for so long, I need a transfusion! I laughed at myself, but really, that is it! A transfusion of what opens the channels to feel. To recover my empathy and the intuition—both of which felt scrambled, making me doubt my own self. I now realize that is a technique of one trying to control another. Instead of worrying about love not flowing from me, let me find a channel, just one to start, regardless of from which direction it flows. Transfusion is the word that keeps coming to me. So, how do I get a transfusion of love? I do not know. So, I narrowed the focus because love is too broad for me. And what does it mean when it is so broad anyway? Deep levels of love so many seek in another person are often not found there. Those levels are like a river. They ebb and flow; they are shallower at times and very deep at others; sometimes with a current, and other times just a rest in a nice eddy of the river; sometimes rapids, and sometimes waterfalls! Cultivate and develop my own river; that is what I need to do. And there is my transfusion. Do any of you feel like you are thirsting for this, or is it just me?

I found an opening to finding my sixth sense again in the most unexpected place. While waiting for the courts to catch up and process the split of income, I was yet to have my half of income. So, I really needed to find a way to supplement while this process goes on. Synchronistic, coincidental, godsent, gift from the universe, or whatever you want to call it; I was asked to babysit a dog. Ugh! Responsibility I really did not want, but still not having learned to say no, I said yes.

A few days turned into 10 days, and during that time, the dog and I had bonded. The dog was a changed dog when he went home with my friend, and now, I am the go-to dog sitter. And she told a few other friends and neighbors, who passed the word about me. People were driving from over an hour away each way for me to have their dogs for a few days or a month. Next thing I know, I have 50-something 5-star reviews and am at times having to turn people down. My heart creaked open when I thought I would be helping the dogs. Each dog in my care gets a full body massage, and I practice animal Reiki, so each has a full session daily. Something magical happens there. It's a channel of love to me and the dogs! And the glacier which froze pathways to the free-flowing love in my heart and soul started little trickles of melting. I did not notice! It is the free-flowing kind I had as a kid.

What brought me the most peace and connection in my past when I had a free flow of feeling, intuition, empathy, connection, and just knowing certain things? I find myself in a stream of consciousness; I stop thinking and listen. What do I hear? I have taken myself where I hear nothing artificial. Birds chirping; the gentle hum of cicadas; my own damn thoughts trying to break into the peace but just keep going, and those thoughts flow away just like the river passing by in front of me. What's left is still the birds chirping, the hum of cicadas, the gentle flow of the water passing by, and now the howl of a monkey in the far jungle background. I just sit with that and listen. It is like a rainforest rhythm, a calming city beat, a splash in a lake, or whatever flows. I realize that so much of what has blocked my healing is continuing the pattern of what helped me survive during the worst of the recent few years. That was closing everything out, even the places where I found peace and connection. I still went there to those physical places, but I just plowed through the motions. I really did not smell the salt air, the fresh pines, and the mountain breeze. The river flowed by, but I was incapable of hearing and feeling it. I had contributed to the choking constriction and stuffed myself back into myself! Consciously I knew that peace, joy, and love lived inside me, but I could just not let anything penetrate. I am in self-protect mode, stopping even what brought me the most peace. Let me out!

I am still a work in progress. I admit that as of writing this, I feel emotionally constipated. It is a major effort to go out and see people when all

I still want is peace and to guard myself. But gradually, I force myself out and make no excuses if I do not go, if I am not confining and barricading myself against the flow, which I know will take me to love. Where I can then begin the broader levels of discovering love again. But first, now that the "vampire" has moved on, and I am free, I can rediscover my own blood and life force. And love will flow freely within me again. Get out that sticky pad and write one thing to start. For me, it was identifying that I was sucked dry by a "love vampire," but that does not mean I cannot have new transfusions to replace what I have lost. I do not need victims or to be a victim to feel genuine and deep levels of love, and that is the blood life force of all of us.

Nature is where I have always found peace and connection. And heights—the higher, the better. I sit below the tree house I helped build but am blocked from accessing and pretend I am looking out from that 60-foot height. This is where it begins for me! Thank you, tree house! I do not have to be in you to feel you. Ha! I built that with all the freedom and pure love and joy I had as a kid. And I can still feel you when I sit beneath you.

Find the place where you, at one time, felt deep love and connection. Maybe it is a city; maybe it is at your grandparent's grave site or in front of where they lived. Maybe it is in a museum. Maybe it is railroad tracks (love those too). Find dogs or animals and love them. Find that love connection wherever you can. I believe this is where the channels begin to open. Feel what you feel; do not cram it down. I cry as I sit here writing because the connection is that strong for me. Do not choke yourself or continue to let a vampire suck you dry even after they are gone. You have had enough of that. Now, it is time to breathe. Do not rush. Sit, feel, and allow what flows to flow. Tears, laughter, joy, dance, walk, whatever. Allow it to move through you as you feel it so you are not holding onto pain and negativity. Do it regularly. I found one day any negativity thrown my way just rolled right off. Some days will be easier than others. See if this helps you. For now, the dogs and I are taking a walk to the river. Be back in a few.

Love, Blondie

About Blondie Rebecca Amelia

 Having overcome a psychologically and physically abusive childhood, Blondie turned those experiences toward helping others overcome their own adversities. Using the skills of organizing and natural sales ability, she moved from the corporate world to Costa Rica, where she lives a significant part of the year.

After college, she moved into sales, where she excelled for many years. Finding herself dissatisfied in this sterile world, she decided to give it all up for something she was passionate about.

Using her organizational skills and corporate world experience, she invites leaders in specialties from the arts to healing (and many in between) to bring groups to her wildlife reserve estate in Costa Rica where they can learn and practice in a safe and private, isolated space during workshops and retreats. As an empath, she is sensitive to her guests and leaders. Also, as a Reiki practitioner, she uses her natural talents in healing and helping people so that those in crisis or stuck can turn their breakdowns into breakthroughs.

Being single in a lush, pristine, and isolated rainforest has not been an easy journey. Doing much of the work herself to turn this amazing and healing place into a space where others can come to heal and learn, she is passionate about providing a safe space for her family, friends, and others.

Blondie currently splits her time between Maine and Costa Rica.

Website: www.corcovadosprings.com
Email: osablondie@gmail.com
LinkedIn: www.linkedin.com/in/osa-peninsula-travel-039b75169

Facebook: Osa Peninsula Travel:
www.facebook.com/OsaPeninsulaTravel
Corcovado Springs:
www.facebook.com/profile.
php?id=100081274152617&mibextid=ZbWKwL
Contributing author, *Mission Hope, Vol. II:*
www.amazon.com/Mission-Hope-Inspirational-Stories-
Triumph

Dear Love Life

—

Hope Blecher Croney

If I had kept a diary for the past 56 years, it might look like this. I recall those diaries with small keys tied with a piece of ribbon. Remember those books hidden under pillows or under the bed? Remember those small keys that were so easy to lose?

Before you continue, allow me to clarify what you are about to read. These entries are not from my actual diaries. Those diaries are buried, collecting dust somewhere. Yet, the feelings and incidents rise up every now and again. What you are about to read, these letters that become words, phrases, and sentences; what are these? These are fictionalized entries that let you travel through my reflections and recollections about love. In between will be some poetry, some imagery, and some other ways that I will convey love and hope.

Thank you for committing to reading this chapter. Now, let us come together to take the first tiny and beautiful step. Let us do it just as Mary Poppins and Bert did when they jumped into those colorful chalk sidewalk pictures in the original Mary Poppins movie. True tidbit, that was the first movie I saw with my mom and friend in a little town in New Jersey, USA.

> *Dear Diary,*
> *What is love? Will I know it when it happens? Will I feel it? What will it look like? Love confuses me.*

Dear Diary,

He loves me; he loves me not. He loves me; he loves me not. How do I know? How will it show?

Dear Diary,

Is love the Fantasticks? Is love a song? Is it a dance? Does it smell like roses? Will I cry like I did when reading about Ma, Pa, and Laura and about Charlotte and Wilbur?

Dear Diary,

Pudgy, chubby, chunky, fat. Glasses and braces and a pixie haircut. Being a good student. Getting good grades. Doing chores. Mowing, picking weeds. Giving out Bazooka. Walking to school. Passing notes. Studying. Friends?

Dear Diary,

I cried. St. Exupery and the Little Prince. I cried. Someone left. Someone died. Is that love?

Dear Diary,

What is love? Is it a twirl on the stage? Is it putting up with every-thing? Is it a touch that has me turning red or giggling?

Dear Diary,

If I am in love, how will I feel? Will I feel less alone? Why do they leave me alone when they find others? Do friends fall out of friendships? Are friends a search for belonging? For love?

Dear Diary,

Someone who loves me will wait for me, right? Someone who loves someone else doesn't make them cry? Lovers don't hit each other, right? Are my parents in love? If so, why is there so much yelling? Why did she walk out? Why is there silence?

Dear Diary,

It is a blur today. The call; the hours in the car. The traffic. The closing of doors. The calls. It's a blur, but it's real. Is there love in death? What happens to love when someone dies?

Dear Diary,
Is love only in the movies? Is it found on vacations in faraway places? Maybe a blue lagoon or a place where there's a rescue during a monsoon? Who will swoon?

Dear Diary,
Off to class again. That dread of coming back to the dorm room. The cackles; the angst. The distant hug lost because I said no. No to intercourse.

Dear Diary,
What is a happy ending? Does love come once in a lifetime? Are there different types of love?

Dear Diary,
Flowers, jewelry, cards, and more. Is that love? Is that how they show love? Is love something tangible? They are still together after 50 years, so let's cheer and forget the tear. Right?

Dear Diary,
Can I be alone in love? That doesn't seem to be right. Can a person be in a room of people and feel alone? If I could see love from outside of myself, what would that look like?

Dear Diary,
Wow, look at that rock! It is huge, and it glistens and glimmers. This wedding is going to be huge.

Dear Diary,
I never saw kisses. I never saw hands being held. I got a kiss on the keppie. I got a smile. Those I can see in my mind. That spot I can touch. Was that their love for me?

Dear Diary,

I don't recall hearing them say "I love you." I wonder if they did love each other or love me. Must saying those words and hearing those words be part of love?

Dear Diary,

I could be a young widow. I dropped everything to get to that hospital. What will happen?

Dear Diary,

Writing, working, driving, carpooling, diapering, calling, buying, returning. Busy; tired. Pausing and becoming a mom, a wife, fitting in, yet wanting something else. Feeling out of sorts; is this feeling in love or falling out of it?

Dear Diary,

I'm not feeling it. She goes every day, almost, to see him. I have flashes of arguments, drive-aways, returns, tears, passing away. Yet, every day …

Dear Diary,

I move away. Each day, a bit more. As he is sick, and as we pray, shouldn't I be feeling the same way? Why don't I feel that commitment? Why don't I feel that I would do the same thing for him?

Dear Diary,

Chit-chat and food. Smiles, hugs. Tears, black.

Dear Diary,

It's time; it's too soon. You'll know when it's the right time. Hands go over my ears. Another wipes away tears.

Dear Diary,

Long hair or short? Lose weight? New clothes? Heels or no heels? Healing?

Dear Diary,

Is there love in fear?

Dear Diary,

Lying, crying, denying while driving, working, and playing.

Dear Diary,

I made the call. I made the appointment. Will I follow through with it? Yes.

Dear Diary,

That next step is a big one. It will change everything. Will people blame me? This is hard. Should I do it? Why or why not?

Dear Diary,

Well, I did it. I got yelled at. They will be lost. You're destroying the family. You're a white trash homewrecker. You are selfish. This is so hard; I am not changing my mind.

Dear Diary,

Why didn't you tell us sooner? Were you abused? They mean physically, I know, and no.

Dear Diary,

Spiritual guidance, spiritual comfort—that does not exist. It is a farce. They dropped like flies. Silence.

Dear Diary,

Lost. Wander. Lost in work.

Dear Diary,

They are okay. They hug me. The magic of dance is helping them. What or who is helping me? The doctor asks. The name changes. What to call myself?

Dear Diary,

Where is the theme song and the score? Where is the happy ending? This is wrong. This is not a song or a movie. This is reality.

Dear Diary,

He lied, and it still hurts. I cursed. I am shaking. That Get got me. He laughed at me. The Rabbi and tribunal at the Bet Din. My blood pressure rose; my voice rose. He will not win! How could he? Head up, Hope.

Dear Diary,

The job is good; the season is changing; the kids are okay. It's a new day.

Dear Diary,

A cat, really? Growing up, it was fish. Divorce, freedom—nope. Divorce, kids, job, driving, writing, smiling, adopting a shelter cat. Okay, why not? How bad could it be? It's returnable, unlike other things in life.

Dear Diary,

Am I worthy of love? Am I pretty? I've lost weight. I've gotten new glasses. Will anyone notice? Is it okay? Has enough time passed?

Dear Diary,

There's a leak, a small flood in the bathroom; it's freezing outside, and he wants to take me out for a delayed New Year's dinner. We can't. Time to clean, wash towels, and … Oh my gosh! The rug is soaked. Ugh!

Dear Diary,

If the kids don't agree, the answer is no. What about my happiness? I'm a mom; they are minors; they come first. My baggage doesn't need to become their weight.

Dear Diary,

Leaving on a jet plane. Fingers crossed for a happy year away from here. We'll see her at the airport with open arms and hugs.

Dear Diary,

This isn't the Brady Bunch. I don't know from that lifestyle of late nights, no curfews, out and about with no responsibilities, dabbling in illegal substances. Into Momma Bear mode—protect the kids and my job. My job that provides stability, health benefits, and pays the bills. My pensionable job. It's who I am and what I do; those are intertwined.

Dear Diary,

The intertwining is not happening. Yup, let's call it a failure. Outplacement treatment, sparse attendance, lots of air freshener, and the like. I am too strict. Does anyone really follow those rules? Yes!

Dear Diary,

I see now that I was played the fool. I provided the house, the food, the driveway, the place to park one's self with one or two teens in tow. The cost? Beyond monetary. Thievery, loss of material items, loss of love, loss of life.

Dear Diary,

What's the cost of love? Isn't it priceless?

Dear Diary,

Yes, a big one. Beautiful setting; lots of people being happy for us. Delicious food. A beautiful dress. The kids being happy for us. POP that bubble.

Dear Diary,

I'm going along with it. Small wedding. Justice of the peace. Heck, I just typed my own wedding license application in this small office in this small town in a new state. How bad could it be?

Dear Diary,

I can back out. I can say no; after all, I did that once before, you know.

Dear Diary,

The happy job rug got swept away. The joy of going to work and creating new learning experiences is gone. The doctor can give me medicine to feel better. I hear her words, "Is this job worth taking medicine for? Here are the side effects ...."

Dear Diary,

So, his passing was a wake-up call. The doctor's words are a wake-up call. Heck, let's sell the house and hitch the trailer up to the truck and drive away. Who cares where; just away. People do that, right?

Dear Diary,

House sold. Boxes moved. This isn't where I wanted to go. It's practical. I thought I could be spontaneous just for once. So predictable. They say counting on me is a strength.

Dear Diary,

Leave it all behind? Pack it all up? Still being the responsible one. Boring? Boring!

Dear Diary,

I want freedom, but those are just words because I don't know what that would even look like. I want to wander. I am not having a breakdown. I've seen that, and this isn't it. I read all those slogans and see those commercials to set up boundaries, to commit to healthy habits, to smile, to do this and that, to set an intention for each day, to meditate. Too much of telling me what to do. Am I so damaged?

Dear Diary,

So much jargon. Frenemies, OMG, LOL, and emojis with hearts, without hearts. What kind of communication is that? What feelings does that convey? It's convenient; it's shorthand; it's quick. Is it authentic?

Dear Diary,

I love you, too. Is that just a reply, an automatic response, or is it for real? Am I trapped again? Can I get out? Do I want to? Are they trapped? Is that smile authentic or hiding something?

Dear Diary,

It happened. The call. The drive to the hospital. It happened again and again and again.

Dear Diary,

Well, well, here we are. Care provider bag packed, ready just in case. Years ago, it was the birthing bag, then the hospital bag for him, and then him, and now for her. I'm getting a bit … what's the word?

Dear Diary,

I'm supposed to appreciate all she's done. Do they? I hear the words spoken about me that maybe I wasn't supposed to hear. "She does so much for them. She's given them so much. What's next for her?" Hello, I am that her.

Dear Diary,

At this age, what's love? I turn back pages and see how many years ago I asked that same question. Love is a four-letter word.

Dear Diary,

Love is a double-edged sword. It hurts. Does it heal? Does it help? Is it necessary or something we're told we can't live without? Hmm, when do I really remember hearing those three words, I love you?

Dear Diary,

Leave me alone. Let me do my thing. Your thing isn't my thing. Stop questioning.

Dear Diary,

I saw the sun today. I saw the full moon. The brightness is calming. The vastness isn't scary.

Dear Diary,
Let me pause here to introduce you to the dear readers.

I write this piece a week after the 15th anniversary of the passing of my father. In my family, people don't die; they pass away. I'm writing this chapter and sharing these fictionalized entries with you as a way to tease out the tangles of love.

In my six decades of life here on Earth, there have been life cycles of natural births and deaths, life cycles of deaths by suicide and symbolic deaths—as some refer to divorce. There have been celebrations of birthdays, anniversaries, and holidays.

In a few boxes in a basement sit engagement photos, ketubahs, birth announcements, greeting cards, and other mementos. I cry; I learn about people that I never met or those that passed through my life. Is keeping them a way to hold onto something that the next generation will just toss away? In this movement to minimize one's belongings, I am not there yet. Do I have to be?

One thing I minimized was love. Is love something I must explain? Is love something I can explain? There are foods I enjoy. There are places I visit and wish to visit. If you love a band, do the musicians care? That is something I see a person I know struggling with as celebrities become outspoken about various topics and also spokespeople for products. There are music groups I like and songs I enjoy listening to, but I don't hop on a plane and make it to their concerts because I love their music. There is also a financial consideration for me too.

Love, for me, is a people-based word. In writing this piece for you, I explored myself. Love wasn't a word I heard. I am told it was something I knew someone else had for me, felt for me. Now, at my current age and stage of life, that assumption, is it enough? I don't want it to be something I'm presumed to know. I want to know without a shadow of a doubt. Did she love me? Did she love me not? I don't want anyone to wonder that about Hope.

I can see it clear as day when I realized that my first marriage was going to end. My dad was in a care facility, and my mom would go almost every day to see him. I looked over at my husband and thought to myself, *I don't see myself doing that for you.* At that minute, I realized that I didn't love him because if I did, come hell or high water, I would know and feel that I would do that for him. Yet, because of my father's health, which to this day I always hoped he would be able to come back home, I didn't run to an attorney, nor did I run away with the kids. It was a slow decline. But when I made the decision, the choice, to this day, I don't regret it. I remember hearing my kids tell their father they love him. It hurt. After x, y, and z, they still say that. They love him in a way that is different from our love. I've come to that space.

I regret giving up on myself. I regret trying to fit into boxes. I am taking steps—tiny, mighty, beautiful steps through which I am speaking up. I am pausing to listen sometimes. I react, respond, and reflect; some say overthink and overdo. I fear letting someone down, and I am not in therapy for that or anything else. It's me; it's Hope. When you get Hope, when I am in a room, I've been told that I have so much to share and make space for so many people in my projects, yet who makes space for me? Is there reciprocity?

Is love reciprocal? Is love magical? Does it dance or smell? Does it have a taste? Does love have a sense? How do you sense love? I've come to a space where I know love isn't a Hallmark movie, a song, or a dance. Love is a feeling, and it's demonstrated and heard in a variety of ways. Yet, younger Hope, little Hope, still hopes that she's correct in assuming that what wasn't spoken was that feeling from those no longer here to speak for themselves for generations past.

Because my parents stayed married for over five decades, does that mean they loved each other? Is love cultural? Is it religious? Is it just it? Parental love for a child. Love for one's job. Love for this and that. My head is spinning.

My hope for you, the reader, is also the next step that I am taking, and here it is in black and white for you and the world. Wow, now I better do it. I am going to take steps to decrease negative self-talk, whether that occurs in my mind, out of a pencil tip, or off my lips. I am going to decrease Disneyfied and Hallmarkian images of love. I am going to take steps to increase my love of myself, as that fits me and feels right for me, Hope. I will take tiny, mighty, Hope-filled steps. Join me and let's embrace the faith, joy, and love of being hopeified.

Thank you for letting me play with words along this journey. Sometimes, being creative feels better than struggling to find words when the exact word isn't in one's dictionary.

Dear Diary and Dear Readers,

Love has as many letters as hope. As long as there is life, there is hope. Here's what I hope: that my kids like themselves. That they have friends who are as devoted to them as they are to their friends. That they have jobs where they feel valued as employees. That they have something to smile about each day. That when they are in pain, the person they count on comes through. That when they come to a bump in the road, it's a detour. That walking away to a better day is a believable option. That one recognizes that staying just because you want to be in love is not obligatory. That the gut-head connection is real. That you know what makes you you and that you can hold onto yourself. That you can find something funny and laugh. That situations do not envelope you. That adjusting to others is not the same as loss of self. That you find the wherewithal to thwart social media from defining you.

Look, at the intersection of our words joy, hope, and love. It is an o. That o, that O, is a circle. It can be a zero, the letter o; it can have a long sound and a short sound. It has a circumference, a radius, and a diameter. It has the ability to roll away and back. It is a mirror image of itself. That o is the world in you.

- Grab a pencil.
- Make an O, o.

126

- Handwrite the j and y, then the u so the words joy and you are connected.
- Add the h and p, the l and v.

Now your rhyming directions are done, just as the setting sun. You are a person. You are a real person. You are a love-worthy, real person. You, joy, hope, and love are connected. Believe!

Thank you for believing in me. Thank you for believing in yourself. Best wishes for your love adventure.

Sincerely,
Hope

About Hope Blecher Croney

 Dr. Hope Blecher is an educator with 39 years of experience spanning grades kindergarten through college. In addition to five earned educational certificates, Hope holds three earned degrees, a BA, an MA, and an Ed.D. Hope has enjoyed years as a classroom teacher, a district supervisor, and a director of curriculum and instruction, in addition to creating and providing professional learning and development workshops. She continues to evolve as an educator through both synchronous and asynchronous educational work.

As a semi-retired teacher, Hope works with adult learners as an instructional coach and a teacher of multilingual learners/English as a New Language learners. From working with students with special needs to her own gifted and talented children and adults in college courses, Hope has encapsulated those experiences in six published books. The topics include activities for celebrating the 100th day of school to engaging students in the joy of writing.

Between her daughter, son, and husband, Hope and her family have an assortment of pets and hobbies. When not writing, Hope is involved in her community as the founder of a nonprofit project, Hope's Compass Fund, at http://www.hopescompass.org, and as a volunteer for various organizations. As her curiosity and creativity guide her, Hope wanders with wonder and connects people and places, arts, literature, and more in new ways.

Hope invites readers to reach out to her to share their wanderings, wonderings, and artings; yes, she is making that a word. She thanks her family and friends for their support. Over the past few years, Hope has come to envelop her given name and embrace it, as people no longer make jokes about it. Now, that name, Hope, is viewed and respected as an asset.

Hope thanks you, the readers, for making the time to follow her on social media, for purchasing and sharing this poetry and prose, and for being kind to one another. Let's be hopeful, provide sanctuary for one another, show compassion, and bridge communities.

LinkedIn: Hope Blecher (Sass), Ed.D. | LinkedIn
Website: www.hope4education.com
Other links: linktr.ee/hope4education

We Were Made For Love

—

Loree Dittrich

Love is patient; Love is kind; Love is not envious or boastful or arrogant or rude. It does not insist on its own way; It is not irritable or resentful: It does not rejoice at wrongdoing but rejoices in the truth. It bears all things, believes all things, hopes all things, endures all things. Love never ends.
—1 Corinth: 13: 4–8

I am unique and wonderfully made. God's love for me is everlasting just as is told to us in Corinthians. "Our" chosen verse for our wedding day. The one I am called to live up to and the one I have at times failed to do. God wants to give us the love we desire and deserve. We were to be gifted to each other ... honored, protected, cherished, crowned with HIS love. That was the plan. God, to me, as the author of my life, is always in control. But as humans and sinners, we don't always follow the plan. I contemplated deeply whether or not I was even worthy to write on the topic of love, as, to me, the greatest love story of all was already written. What could I possibly add to the Almighty's whose love and peace pass all understanding?

My awareness brings me to know that there are many ways to express and impress love upon others. There is God's way, and there is our way. And we spend lifetimes trying to share and prove and glorify "OUR" love. And for the millions of love stories shared, every love story has a beginning and an ending. For some, it is happy. For some, it is sad. For me, I dream of the "everlasting" love story where God gets the glory. My truth is that I believe in a love that I am not even capable of. A love that I strive for, I'm alive for, and Christ died for. It is a love that is higher and stronger and lasts longer than what is humanly possible. I believe that love and faith are dependent on God's truth over our speculation. Love is within reach, yet beyond reach. Possibly unattainable and unexplainable, but I'll give it a try. And the first thing I've had to become for love is vulnerable—and trustful.

Love is vulnerable

Love is taking off your mask in front of others, and they in return love you for what you truly are! The depths of our love depend on the confines of our minds. Love is an emotion of positivity triggered by appeal ... Love is real! Love spirals when it feels understood. And if God seems far away, who moved? It is always the US!

For He so loved the world ... Loving is forgiving the unforgivable; otherwise, you will never be at peace. Be bold; let love unfold. We are love bearers. We are all hungry for love to quench our thirst. Life is love, and all our love is passed down for generations to come. No act of love ever exists without gain. In the end, loving is surrendering and letting go, whether by choice or circumstance. Why prolong suffering? Why hang on to what is not yours? Why the attachments? All things pass as my mother recently reminded me when I went to visit her and take food on Christmas day. Yes, Mother, but...

> There is something
> About the legacy of
> A mother's precious love
> That outshines all others
> A million golden stars
> Twinkling above.
> —Loree Dittrich

Love is work, and servanthood matters. There is no end to the work of love. Life starts with a "labor" of love, which devoted parents continue with. Unmarried people fulfill doing what they love or careers for passion's sake too. Love is to flourish, to nourish, and to have a sense of belonging. It is a safe harbor. It does not enable. It is the bow that is stable, bringing fruits of virtue to the table. Love is empowering. It is demonstrated by small acts of love.

When we seek and lean into love, it is also the healer of afflictions. This intoxicated love means we mustn't let the sun go down upon our wrath. Yet how often have we done that? Marital discord or any chord that is not in harmony is unrelated to love. Disrespect, disconnect, and fear especially do not exemplify love. Love is not fear-based. "Perfect Love casts out fear." For me, I've had work to do in this regard. To say I was always coming from a place of love would be a lie. I confess to having failed miserably at love, not in defining love but living up to love.

Afflictions are often just reasons to increase our faith and love. Without knowing the value of love and forgiveness; I would be a crushed grape that never made it to the sparkling wine—a grape of wrath! However, I fully understand the two key elements that the Lord came to teach us, which are love and forgiveness.

I accept that love is forgiving and enduring, and I have also learned that sometimes love is stronger in absence or death, for "Love is stored in the soul's memory. Love spirit lives on and transcends life!" Rise above with love! Breathe on ... and hopefully, in this breathing space, you will find room and desire to grow and reaffirm. To me, being in love and growing in love is never exclusive outside of God's love. For love trusts and finds confidence in God's providence. I dream of a world where every human being is cherished and gets the love that they are worthy of. Love needs connection and conversation where people feel a sense of belonging to a family or a community.

Brief, our
Time on Earth
Will be - Don't
Spend it all

Astray - God's
Greatest desire
For us all - Is
That we live
In communion
Each day
—Loree Dittrich

When life and love are misunderstood, the grace of God and His undying love will speak to you in mysterious ways. It enlightens me to think that love is probably the most powerful force on Earth. I am grateful for that love and the many gifts it has blessed me with along the way through its significance and miraculous ways. Some of my fondest are the births of our four daughters and holding these little scrunched faces, sleepy-eyed bundles of love in my ever-ready arms. It was love at first sight with these tiny miracles of creation that would change my life forever. Feelings of gratitude and joyfulness flooded me. A feeling of being needed. A love surge! That giving and receiving through the life of a child. Are babies not the sweetest, purest form of love on the planet? To these lives, you add hope, faith, and love in the process. When you are a confident, caring mother, your children feel it. They have grown up now and have families of their own, and they have made me proud.

Also, to my family and friends, for their love and for showing up in times of need.

To my husband, for all the ways he's tried to surprise me and care for me in ways that mattered!

Love fuels human kindness and reinforces that safe feeling that comes over us during life's storms. It is credibility. It is creativity. It is helping people to find new and traditional ways to love. It is helping those who struggle to restore faith in humanity. Faith permeates love. Pure love ideally is holiness. Holiness equals the perfection of charity. The utterance of scripture is there to assist us and fill our cups.

With love, we strive to work with intention toward love's purpose. In times of distress, we must work harder. "Love is going to battle; giving it your all—answering the call." Battles fought—lessons taught. Love is unselfish and will disappear almost completely without effort and going the extra mile. A life devoid of love needs to be reviewed and renewed with its spirit. I think back to a song we girls sang in CGIT, "They'll Know We Are Christian By Our Love" (under the guidance of my dear friend, Eileen, who I kept in touch with until she died in her 90s). To succeed in love, we have to lift our whole being up and those around us too. Eileen mastered that! And my friend Alma at 95, who calls me and always seems to have my back. Oh, for the love of seniors!

The second commandment reminds us of "one love," united and universal. We are also to be obedient and stay humble, ridding ourselves of that which makes us stumble. We are to keep the random love that is filled with kind words and gestures and touches others. We do this without hesitation when we are in God's hands, which is a great place to be. Scripture shows us Jesus was patient, present, and filled with love. He died for love. The message is clear. Love is sacrificial and unconditional, and we are loved with an everlasting love. And this is a love both human and divine. It is unchanging and merciful. We, too, when inflamed with this love can respond with love. Blessed St. Teresa penned, "Love is in season at all times and within the reach of every hand." She also penned, "Do small things with great love"... and many more that I love.

In my younger married life, we were told at a retreat love is a decision. I remember that making great sense to me. My life, for the most part, has been used to try and make a difference in the world. By deciding to love, I've also embraced the ripple effect of love, which sustains me. Call it ripple; call it reciprocal—as in the Moulin Rouge line, "The greatest thing you will ever learn is just to love and to be loved in return."

Love breathes life into you. Love is energy. Love makes us feel worthy and noble. To know love is to grow in love. It's like a seed in good soil. It propagates. It's that unseen universal force, as our love links us together. We were made for love. Here's another quote I read that I cannot get out of my head: "Your love does for me what stained glass does for a window ..." Or how about "Do you love me because I'm beautiful, or am I beautiful because you love me"?

Love can also mean letting go of those not meant for you or deserving of your love. Look within instead. Turn the key and unlock the love that lies waiting for you. There, too, comes a time ... we must purge ourselves of all the fluff and stuff and be rid of unnecessary attachments—all that clutters your gutters. Let it go. Free the flow.

I feel as though I am learning about love even as I write this, for I'm reliving it and reviewing it as I pen my way to completion. Love at its best means having someone or something to share it with. Dates and money spent on "two-togetherness" build up foreverness. Love is showing concern for your lover or another's well-being when the chips are down ... through a job loss, a drop in salary, a tough year, a major life crisis when your child's report card is not up to your expectations, or when your challenging child becomes more challenging, or you just do not seem able to muster enough strength for the task. This is where love comes down. This is where love is the ointment that needs to be applied—where love helps and heals and makes things better; where the language spoken is your love language; where nothing on Earth can do it quite like love!

Love is:
Forgiving myself
For those times
I failed to reach out
When my arms
Weren't long enough
And my heart
Wasn't strong enough.
—Ld.

Love always hopes for the best, while faith endures each test!

Quotes I Wrote:

- *By relying on God's grace, hope, and mercy, hearts are changed, and lives move forward.*

- *Lord, teach us to love—when dark clouds hang over, and resentment overrides our happiness; when our blessings become cursing, and our spirits are tarnished.*

- *Love is choosing our battles, relying on God's grace, strength, and love.*

- *God's love is limitless, unconditional, sacrificial, and sacred.*

- *No greater love*

- *No greater pain*

- *No greater loss*

- *No greater pain*

- *Couple love is a covenant based on commitment. It is building a future together with another. It is awareness of your partner ... appreciating them and respecting them. It's been said that love is not seeing the right partner. It is being the right partner.*

- *Faith and love mean feeling OK when things don't go your way ...*

> *Here's to those times when I*
> *Feel hollow—And life is hard*
> *To swallow—When my heart*
> *Bleeds, with unmet needs*
> *When the curtains are pulled*
> *As the world closes in on me*
> *When those late-night*
> *Conversations with God*
> *Are the only place to go*
> *When testy times arrive*

And I am not ready for them

But my faith and prayers
Remain—As I wade in
The waters of God's mercy
And his unending
Faith, hope, and love

LOVE

Maybe It's More about:

The simple little things
Kindness that heals
Meaningful words spoken
Laying in the sun on a
Warm sunny day, warmed
By God's incredible love
Being aware of the
Happiness evoked by
Making great choices
And having a joyful spirit
That lights up a room
Maybe it's about loving
And trusting in the process
And knowing that there IS
A God that loves each and
Every one of us
Unconditionally!

More Loree Quotes:

- *Our love is orchestrated as much by our actions as our words.*

- *Love is an emotion, not meant to be an emotional rollercoaster. Get off that ride ASAP. Be mindful of each other's emotions, knowing that feelings come and go, but God's love has staying power!*

- *Love is obedient, responsive, caring, and sharing. Love is showing up when you'd rather not.*

- *Love is clinging to faith with a clear conscience. This you take with you everywhere you go.*

- *Love is choosing your battles, relying on God's grace, strength, and love. Love differs for all.*

- *Love should never be in the form of stealing time from God and family.*

- *The BIGGER person always looks at the bigger picture and sees the best optimum outcome regarding Love.*

- *Living with an open mind and loving with an open heart is the best way to live out the great commandment, whether it be familial love, marriage, or the poor and the oppressed. We never really know for certain what the person sitting next to us is going through.*

- *Loves music is the symphony of the angels. It's a little piece of heaven gifted early.*

- *I strongly believe that love is justice. When love is present, justice prevails. "Love thy neighbor as thyself." The distinction is clear. It leaves little room for error. Being self-righteous or hateful is wrong. Judging is not loving. Acceptance and inclusion are!*

- *There is no magic formula to win at love.*

- *Choosing love is always the right choice, for love is of God, and we were created for love.*

- *If you encounter someone unloved, give them some of yours. Love heals, transforms, and restores worthiness.*

- *We must wear love like a life jacket to preserve us.*

Love is unique for every living person. It is universal, eternal, and available. It is passion, devotion, and emotion. It's a newborn's soft skin. It's your pet's unconditional love and warmth beside you. It's the smell of fresh air after a rain. It's a letter in the mail. Its flowers are delivered with a message of adoration. It's the music in your soul. Your ultimate goal. It's a stop at your favorite destination. It's freshly baked goods. It's a walk in the woods. It's a garden of gratitude. It's intimacy (into me see). It's being in an ocean of wonder. It's warmth at the end of a cold day. It's peacefulness. It's silence. It is being in touch and alone with your loving thoughts. It's knowing your self-worth and not looking outside of yourself for love and approval. It's fondness; it's adoration; it's fashion infatuation; a spa day ridding yourself of inflammation. Love refined and defined—in countless ways since the beginning of time.

For the Christian, the recipe consists of faith, hope, and love; meaning faith in God, hope for the future, and love for all—as in God's love. The love for all is hard, but I beg the question: "Who among you has not at some point struggled with love and fallen short of the glory of God?" And the truth is:

Love for all would advance humanity. Why? WE WERE MADE FOR LOVE. Imagine ridding ourselves of all past grievances—introducing empathy and squashing judgment! It would promote world peace among the nations. It would not only aid us in life but in death and letting go. Really! So, what are we waiting for?

Not sure, but I'm in for a faith and hope that frees me from the bondage of sin and a love that lights my path and is sparked from within. Love is the greatest of all virtues. Love is another word for God. Love is having faith in the continuum of life.

If love is the greatest gift ever received, then let's pay it forward in our actions and our lives. I'll leave you with a blessing once bestowed upon me that stayed with me and encompasses all.

Wishing you unwavering faith, constant hope, and "love" that endures to the end.

Lovingly,
Loree

About Loree Dittrich

 Loree Dittrich lives in Calgary, Alberta, aka the gateway to the Rocky Mountains. She has been writing since the days of her diary and enjoys inspiring others through her many works of poetry, essays, short stories, quotes, funeral poetry, happy mail, and more. Writing is her way in and her way out of herself. Penning her way through life, Loree feels, is truly a huge part of her legacy and most definitely a gift from God.

She is eternally grateful for the four beautiful daughters and nine amazing grandchildren that she and her husband, Bob, have been blessed with, as well as her family and friends who have journeyed with her along the way.

Loree spends three months per year living in Ecuador and has enjoyed the luxury of travel, but it always leads her home—home with her family—and at home in her heart is always a great place to be. Mission "Love" sums it up for her!

Loree is also the author of two children's books, *No Home For A Pigeon* (2019) and *A Boy is Not a Kitten* (2022), and co-author of *Mission Hope, Volume II*.

She looks forward to releasing her many pieces of poetry and others in the future. You may further follow her on:

Instagram: @loreedittrich
Linkedin: Biz Cat 360 Nation (featured contributor)
The Writer's Cafe: (LinkedIn)
E-mail: loreefollowyourdreams@gmail.com

Gaslighting in the Name of Love!

Deborah A. Griffiths

What is love? Is it an emotion? A feeling? An action? Or? This question on love is similar to when Pontius Pilate asked Jesus, "What is truth?" Webster's Dictionary has several definitions for "love," depending upon the word's use as a noun or a verb. There can be a parent's love for a child or the love one friend may have for another out of deep respect and concern for their overall well-being. The definition most of us think of when we hear the word love is "attraction based on sexual desire: affection and tenderness felt by lovers."

Growing up in the '60s and the product of many Disney movies like "Cinderella," it was easy to characterize love as one where the knight in shining armor comes and sweeps the girl off her feet. I know I used this to create my checklist for finding "Mr. Right." The thought of being swept off your feet sounds so romantic. Imagine my surprise when this prince showed up at my door one day. Except this prince came in riding on a dark horse. I didn't know it at the time.

When I met my prince, I was 18 and a freshman in college. Prince Charming approached me on the second day of class to ask for my notes. Imagine my surprise when I saw this tall, dark, and handsome fellow looking at me and inquiring about my notes. We chatted until it was time to go to our classes. Later that afternoon, we saw each other on campus and continued our conversation. One thing led to another, and we began dating. Things were good, or so I thought. He was checking off all my boxes. Tall—check. Good-looking—check. Smart—check. Potential to be a good provider—check. Kind and courteous—check. Behaved like a gentleman—check. Believed in God—check. Prince Charming and I dated for a year and a half before marrying. For the most part, the courtship was typical, except for what I now know was a big red flag. I didn't see it and wasn't even aware of red flags in relationships.

Before our morning classes, we would meet in the parking lot, and Prince Charming would come over and sit with me in my car. We would talk and listen to music before it was time to go to class. One day, he did not get out of his vehicle or even look at me. As the time approached to get to class, I left my car. He subsequently opened his car door and got out. I said hello, and he ignored me. He wouldn't even look at me. I asked what was wrong, but he didn't respond and kept walking. I went on to class. Later that day, I caught up with him on campus and asked him what was wrong. His response was, "You should know." I replied that I didn't know or understand what I could have done wrong to upset him. He proceeded to tell me that I should be the one to get out of my car and go to him, at least occasionally, and that he was doing all the work. I was stunned. I asked him why he didn't say anything about it if it bothered him so much.

I can't fix something I don't know about. Prince Charming scoffed at me and went on about his way. I remember going and buying a card and writing inside the card how sorry I was for upsetting him. The following day, when I saw him pull into the parking lot, I exited my vehicle and walked toward his car. He opened the door, and I gave him the card. And as the old saying goes, we kissed and made up. Years later, as the marriage ended, I came across dozens of cards I gave him—where my first words were "I'm sorry."

A few months after our wedding, Prince Charming was working, and I was in our apartment alone. Out of the blue, there was an earthquake, and I was scared. Although I'm a native Californian, no one ever gets used to these "shakers." I called my family to see if they were okay, and that's when Prince Charming opened the door, asked me who I was talking to, and motioned for me to get off the phone when he heard it was my family. He was outraged that I reached out to my family. He began yelling at me, slapped me in the face, and then punched a hole in the wall. I was stunned. I had not seen this anger before, much less anyone ever exhibiting anger to this extent. Prince Charming apologized, said he would never hit me again, and repaired the wall. He may have fixed the wall, but he couldn't heal my psyche.

The next couple of years, I would describe it as somewhat routine. Prince Charming was working to get his bachelor's degree while I worked a 9–5 job. One day, he invited me to go with him to the desert. I was on vacation that week and didn't feel like going, but he insisted. As we were making our way back home, a car made an illegal U-turn and broadsided us, hitting the vehicle we were in on the front passenger side. I was ejected from the car and suffered two broken kneecaps as well as many cuts and scrapes. Some of the cuts on my face required suturing, and the doctor stitched me up without anesthesia. I was lucky to be alive. Prince Charming walked away from the accident with just a few cuts and bruises. The first responders transported me to the nearest hospital, and he went home. I was alone and scared—even to the point of feeling abandoned. I wondered what I had done to deserve this. The truth is that I had done nothing wrong. I was just in the wrong place at the wrong time and now had an opportunity to make lemonade from these lemons.

After several surgeries and a year and a half of physical therapy, I was walking normally again. During the healing process, I became pregnant with my first child—a son! He became my focus to persevere through physical therapy to get well. I knew he needed a mother who could adequately take care of him. On the other hand, Prince Charming was elated that he had a son, especially one that favored him. Life was good for the next couple of years. Prince Charming was busy climbing the corporate ladder while I stayed home to care for our son. I had discussed going back to work but was told that it was more important to ensure the house was clean, our son was cared for, food was on the table, and his shirts were laundered and pressed. In addition, we moved a couple of times across the country, as he preferred to be closer to his family on the East Coast. I later realized that this distance was a way to isolate me from my family further.

We eventually returned to the West Coast, and our second son arrived. This one favored me in appearance. Imagine my shock when Prince Charming looked at our new son and stated, "He doesn't look like me; how am I going to explain this?" I was hurt. It didn't take long before the oldest son became Prince Charming's favorite. I did what I could to balance things out. It was not easy.

During this time, I was busy with the two boys. He commented on my cooking, appearance, and keeping up the house. I was not allowed to wear nail polish. Should I have any on, he immediately told me to remove it. At the time, the comments seemed trivial and insignificant. But as I would later learn, there's only so much one can take.

My oldest began preschool when I became pregnant with our third child. One day, my son came home with a note from the teacher. Yes, it was one of those notes about behavior. Typical kid stuff! On the other hand, Prince Charming took great offense and, to my surprise, called our son upstairs into the bathroom and began hitting him with a belt. When I realized what was happening, I burst open the door. The beating stopped, but the welts and bruises had begun forming. I was sickened by the whole thing.

I had a hard time sleeping that night. For the first time in the marriage, I contemplated leaving. But here I was, six months pregnant, with no job, no place to go, and no one to call. I was scared to say anything to Prince Charming, as I didn't know how he would take it and if it would lead to another physical outburst. I stayed silent.

A few months later, our daughter was born, and we moved back to the east coast. Prince Charming traveled quite a bit this time and was gone for a week. I took on more household duties, such as lawn mowing, to keep things up. When Prince Charming came home, he spent time with our oldest child or was downstairs, "working" in the basement. He isolated himself more and more from the other two children and me. His demeanor became more critical, and sex was more "on demand" on his terms, including waking me up at 2:00 in the morning. It's not the romanticized version of Prince Charming on the white horse I once imagined all those years ago.

The beginning of the end came about when one of the kids had pneumonia and passed it on to me. I didn't realize it until I woke up one night sweating profusely, with a high temperature, and feeling lousy. Prince Charming was on a camping trip with our oldest son, and when I called him to tell him I was sick, he yelled at me for interrupting the camping trip. I asked a neighbor to watch the other two kids, and I drove myself to the hospital. I stayed in the hospital for a few days. It was an ordeal.

Also, around this time, one of my wisdom teeth became impacted, and I opted to have the remaining three wisdom teeth pulled. The procedure went fine, and I cleaned the house that afternoon. I was doing well, or so I thought, until Monday when I became severely light-headed to the point of passing out. The dental office informed me that it was the after-effect of the anesthesia for the procedure and that I should have rested all weekend. I didn't tell her about the expectations Prince Charming had of me cleaning the house, as the company was soon coming. By the way, he didn't help with the housework. At this point, my physical health impacted my mental well-being, and I no longer wanted to get up in the morning. I began to see a psychiatrist who soon prescribed some anti-depressants. I was spiraling out of control faster than the antidepressants could kick in to balance my levels out. By this time, I believed the only way out was to commit suicide, so I took some pills, thinking that would do me in. It didn't. I woke up many hours later in the psych ward, where my psychiatrist told me, in no uncertain words, "Your environment is making you sick." Those words packed a punch.

I knew then that I had to end the marriage. I wanted my kids to see a strong woman as their mother, and I didn't want them to become victims of abuse or abuse others. Leaving the marriage was not easy. I entered the union while young, believing that marriage lasted until "death do us part." I didn't want it to end with me dying and being in my current state of depression.

I never looked back when I left with the younger two children, as the oldest chose to live with his father. Was I scared to do it on my own? Yes. I also knew that I could do it because the alternative of going back, becoming depressed and suicidal, was not an option. I didn't know how to do it, but I would forge a path, and I did. While raising the younger two children, I found my way back to California to be closer to my family, put myself through school, earned a bachelor's degree, and moved up the corporate ladder myself. As they say, where there's a will, there's a way!

I later learned that what I experienced is known as gaslighting. In 2022, this word, gaslighting, was the most researched word according to Merriam-Webster Dictionary. But what is gaslighting? Merriam-Webster defines gaslighting as the "psychological manipulation of a person usually over an extended period that causes the victim to question the validity of their thoughts, perception of reality, or memories and typically leads to loss and confusion, loss of confidence and self-esteem, the uncertainty of one's emotional or mental stability, and a dependency on the perpetrator." The term "gaslighting" comes from the 1944 George Cukor film, *Gaslight*, starring Ingrid Bergman and Charles Boyer, where the man (Boyer) tries to convince his wife (Bergman) that she is going insane by dimming the gas lights and telling her that it is in her imagination. As a result, she begins to doubt herself and her reality.

According to recent estimates by the Centers for Disease Control and Prevention, "More than 43 million women and 38 million men will experience mental or emotional abuse by an intimate partner." Victims are from all walks of life—race, creed, and color. It knows no boundaries. If you, or someone you know, may be experiencing domestic abuse, please get in touch with the National Domestic Violence Awareness Hotline at 1-800-799-SAFE.

Now, to revisit my original question—what is love? One might think that with my experience, I would be bitter and lonely or maybe even wonder if I believe that love exists. The good news is that I am not bitter; my life is complete, and I still believe in love. But my checklist has changed. Experience taught me that! I do believe in the love a parent has for a child. With three kids of my own, we have been through thick and thin together. We have each other's back, and we know there is nothing we wouldn't do for each other if we could feasibly do it.

Romantic love? Yes, I believe there is a "Mr. Right." But he looks different now, as my checklist has changed. So, "Don't Go Breaking My Heart» and "Stop! In the Name of Love."

My list now looks like this …

1. A man with a heart for God—waiting to check it off.

2. A man with a heart for his spouse—waiting to check it off.

3. A man with a heart for his family — waiting to check it off.

4. A man who has faced adversity and is not bitter—waiting to check it off.

5. A man who is intelligent with a great sense of humor and adventure—waiting to check it off.

I don't know if "Mr. Right" is out there yet for me, but I trust God will provide, should He deem that is His will for my life. And speaking of God; do you want to know what real love is? Look no further than God Himself. He is truth, and He is love. The words in 1 Corinthians 13:4–13 sum up best what love truly is: "Love is patient, love is kind. It does not envy, it does not boast, it is not proud. It does not dishonor others, it is not self-seeking, it is not easily angered, it keeps no record of wrongs. Love does not delight in evil but rejoices with the truth. It always protects, always trusts, always hopes, always perseveres.

"Love never fails. But where there are prophecies, they will cease;

where there are tongues, they will be stilled; where there is knowledge, it will pass away. For we know in part, and we prophesy in part, but when completeness comes, what is in part disappears. When I was a child, I talked like a child, I thought like a child, I reasoned like a child. When I became a man, I put the ways of childhood behind me. For now, we see only a reflection as in a mirror; then we shall see face to face. Now I know in part; then I shall know fully, even as I am fully known.

"And now these three remain: Faith, Hope, and Love. But the greatest of these is Love."

Whether or not you found the love of your life, the words from 1 Corinthians are a great tool to use in all our relationships—work, family, friends, and spouses. Imagine what our world would be like if we all learned to love more!

About Deborah A. Griffiths

 Deborah A. Griffiths was born and raised in the greater Los Angeles area. She graduated with honors from Biola University with a Bachelor of Science degree in Organizational Leadership. This degree helped her advance in the homeowners association industry, where she has written several articles on common interest developments.

Always trying to broaden her horizons, Deborah chose to write her first bestselling novel revolving around the trauma inflicted by gaslighting. This novel is a fictionalized story of a woman's quest to successfully rebuild her life with grace and courage following a painful divorce where she was a victim of domestic abuse. Her follow-up bestselling book, *Open Up – A Guide for Every Woman Who Has Been Abused, Rejected, and Isolated to Write Her Story, Find Her Purpose and Create the Life and Business of Her Dreams* is designed as a guide to recognize red flags and provide steps for rebuilding your life.

With a profound belief in the transformative power of faith, Deborah collaborated in the very successful book *Mission Hope, Volume II,* which became a #1 bestseller. In addition, she also collaborated on a faith-based devotional, *Joy 365.*

Debbie is the proud mother of three grown children and considers her faith and family most important. She enjoys reading, needlework, genealogy, and playing "at" golf in her spare time.

The Power of Love

—

M. L. Sutton

"No emotion, surely, is as cherished and sought after as love." Yet on occasions such as Valentine's Day, we can often be misled into thinking that it consists solely in the swooning, star-crossed romance of falling deeply "in love." But on reflection, love is far more complex. Indeed, arguably, no word covers a wider range of feelings and experiences than love. So how can we ever define what love really is? —Tim Lomas, Lecturer in Applied Positive Psychology, University of East London

Most of us would like to think that we know all there is to know about love, but I think we would be amazed by the amount of difficulty in being able to define it if asked to do so. I'll even go one step further and state that I don't think that it is possible for any of us to really understand the meaning of love until we discover the ultimate depth of God's love. I don't know how it could be possible. And in doing so, it changes our entire way of life, beginning with our heart and how it relates to love and others.

For years, I had thought that I had a reasonable understanding of what love was, though there had always been some confusion for me between the types of love. I've often, as we all have, heard others and maybe even ourselves say that we loved this or that; whether it be ice cream, a family member, a pet, or something in between, even vehicles and recreational items. But I didn't, and those around me often misunderstood me when I stated that I didn't love this, that, or them (meaning individuals I didn't know, though I cared what happened to them).

I had always felt that there must be something more, something to distinguish the degrees between the types or levels of love, never knowing until recently that they were just not in our English language. You see, other languages around our world have varying words to describe each degree of love. For example, the Greeks have seven levels or degrees to differentiate their love:

- Eros: Love of the body. This type of love illustrates sexual attraction and a physical desire toward others and a lack of control. It is powerful, passionate, and can dissipate quickly.

- Philia: Affectionate love. This type accounts for the love that you feel for parents, siblings, family members, and close friends.

- Storge: Love of the child. This type of love describes the unconditional love that parents feel for their children. Unconditional approval, acceptance, and sacrifice defined it.

- Agape: Selfless love. Agape love represents universal love. Greek philosophers felt that this is the type of love that people feel for other humans, for nature, and for a higher power.

- Ludus: Playful love. Love defined by flirtatiousness, seduction, and sex without commitment.

- Pragma: Long-lasting love is evident in couples who have been together for a long period. This type of love continues to develop throughout the years and portrays synchronization and balance. This type of love can only survive with constant maintenance and nurturance.

- Philautia: Love of the self is about realizing confidence and self-worth and is necessary for a sense of purpose and fitting in. (Information gathered from counseling.com.)

The Russians, on the other hand, have only one word for love; however, there are many more ways to say love (in Russian, depending on the context of the sentence and the social setting). The French, often considered as having the flowing language of love, take a different stance on this subject altogether by considering love a fantasy, furthering this idea through their use of poetry, with each poem used as a way to describe one of their seven stages of love. They identify their stages as Admiration, The Physical, Hope, The Birthplace, Crystallization, Reservations, and WTF Just Happened?

As stated in an article by Study.com, titled French Love Phrases, "The French are groomed to think about love from an early age, not in the absolutes of total love or utter rejection, but in nuances and a range of possibilities." The Literary Hub, in their article dated June 29, 2016, say that the French, in particular, make a point of maintaining and analyzing this fantasy. From Abbé Prévost's 18th-century novel of love-drunk obsession to Amélie's quirky quest for romance; from kissing with tongue to Roland Barthes' structuralist critique of the language of love. The 19th-century writer Stendhal explored the complexities and depths of love with unmatched enthusiasm in both life and literature, and while experiencing the highs and lows of it, he declared, "The greatest happiness love can give is the first squeeze of the hand of a woman one loves."

Probably about now, you're wondering why this was such a hang-up of mine; so, I'll tell you. I could never associate the love I felt for my wife with even that toward our children, as close as they were and are to me. But even harder for me was trying to make a connection between them and a vehicle or ice cream. I just couldn't make it work. Over the years, I always held my wife on a pedestal, not to be worshiped but because she was special to me as are our children.

Our children always knew that I loved them and put no one or anything above them other than their mother, and that was the way it had to be for me. Over the years, my love grew for our family and my wife as did my wife's and our children's. We all knew that we each played an integral part and had our own place in our family circle. But in late 2017, our world suffered a major fault. Yes, like that associated with an earthquake. Our lives felt as if they were crumbling, coming apart, with the emergency suffered by my wife—the mortar that held the building blocks of our home and lives together.

It was during a month of daily trips and visits to the hospital and home again each night while being there for my wife—even though she didn't know it—that I discovered a depth of love I'd never thought about or could have assumed possible but found myself to possess. Until this point, I had always known that there was a special bond between us. One that made me want to live again; to see each sunrise while holding her hand in mine; to share each starry night, knowing that she felt secure in the arms that held her close to my side. One that allowed us to finish each other's sentences while marveling at our similar thoughts, as they occurred in unison and allowed us to feel each other's presence when our eyes were none the wiser.

Having had nothing prior to meeting her, I never needed to worry about losing anything, so I lived life haphazardly. But in my late teens, God shook things up by giving me a treasure, and although I didn't understand why, I clung to it, to her, tightly, like a pauper having been given a gem. A gift I knew the value of, or so I had thought, and have since been grateful for in my life.

While at the hospital each day, on the road, and at home each night, I prayed endlessly for her while not seeing what I thought was progress, never giving thought to the fact that God loved her even more than I did or that He already had a rescue plan in place—one I could not see; one that was not only to be about healing my wife's body but also about using her illness as a way to reach me. But this night was different. I knew what I wanted most in life and in that moment, and that was for her life to be spared.

On my way home after a long stint of watching medical teams endlessly trying to help her, only to see their attempts fail, I cried out to the only One whom I knew could help. I remember how deep, heartfelt sobs and moments of breathlessness came over me, while waves of tears washed down my face, momentarily blinding me to the traffic on the road as I asked God to please save her, to take any years that I might have remaining and give them to her. And if it meant that I couldn't be there to see her healing, so be it; I was willing to make that trade. Life and God had been good to me since meeting her. I had enjoyed a beautiful 40 years, spending time with a wife that I could have only hoped would come along for me one day, and I had enjoyed sharing the pleasures of having and helping raise two of the finest children into adulthood, and I was proud of it all. But I was willing to give it all up for her to live.

I had been raised in a Christian home, and I knew about God and His Son, Jesus Christ. And I knew of what He had done for me by hanging on the cross at Golgotha. As a young child, I had accepted Him as my personal savior. But I was no longer that young child, and life and I had tangled a few times over the years. I knew where I was going when I died and gave no thought to death, although I also knew what "making it by the skin of one's teeth" meant, and I knew I could do better. To my way of thinking, if I was asking God for a favor, one as big as this one, then I should be willing to do my part by being the best I could be for however long that it might be, which I knew meant rededicating my life to His will and use, and I did it there and then while driving.

I felt a peace come over me instantly, one that I had not felt in some time, letting me know that God had heard my prayers. No longer was I worried about my wife's health and safety. Concerned? Yes, but not worried. I didn't know what God was going to do with the favor I had asked of Him, but I knew it would work out for the best if I left it in His hands, and I did.

On seeing the light of day the next morning, it appeared as if God had been awaiting me to make a decision the night before. Was I going to come to Him with what seemed to be one of the biggest requests of my life or continue to think I could handle things on my own? (A passage of scripture comes to my mind as I write this—Jeremiah 29:11–14, "For I know the thoughts that I think toward you, says the Lord, thoughts of peace and not of evil, to give you a future and a hope. Then you will call upon Me and go and pray to Me, and I will listen to you. And you will seek Me and find Me, when you search for Me with all your heart. I will be found by you, says the Lord, and I will bring you back from your captivity.") Though the night had been a short one, the morning revealed that the previous six hours had proved to be a turning point not only for my wife but for me as well.

While I was driving to the hospital, just as I was going through the traffic light in a nearby town, my phone rang, and on answering it, I heard the receptionist give the name of the hospital and then lost reception, and I panicked. It was too early for them to be on station (the previous eight days had not been good). Just the day before, the doctors had told me that they had tried everything, and nothing was working to get my wife off the ventilator. I had watched them each day trying, and I understood what they were saying. One doctor had told me that there was a medicine no longer in use, but if they could find it, they would try it, but if not able to locate it, or it didn't work, this morning, it was over.

I pulled off into a local market parking lot, with my body inside and out quivering in spasms. I called them back, expecting the worst, but at that same moment, a song titled "Breathe" came on the radio, and I took a breath just as if having been told to do so. The ICU receptionist told me they had gotten my wife off the ventilator, and she was doing well. Right then, it was as if all the hours of repeated worrying, praying, and begging over those three weeks had built an invisible dam, and it had just blown apart, releasing the largest surge of stored-up adrenalin and anxiety ever to be released. (To this day, I believe it was God telling me to take a breath because I was truthfully running out of air because of sobbing so hard). When I regained my breath, I thanked God for giving her back to me. And as much as I wanted to get there to see her, I couldn't leave until I could see well enough and calm the shaking down enough to drive.

When I got up to the ICU that morning, she was sitting up in bed, smiling at me the way she always had—with that soft "come hither" look, the one that always warmed my heart. Though looking a little worse for wear, she was a beautiful sight to behold. With many of the machines and lines connecting her to them gone, and doctors and nurses scurrying about her, as much as I wanted to just run to her and hold her, I stood out of their way. And while standing there, looking at her from a distance and soaking in the beauty of her smile, I felt as though my insides were melting. It was a beautiful thing to see my wife's eyes wide open again and her smile back.

You might ask, "What has all this to do with the power of love?" I'll tell you, had it not been for my love for my wife, I may not have found my way back to Christ. I fully believe, and always will, that God's intentions were to heal her from the beginning and allow us additional time together as a family. But I didn't know or think about it the previous night. While on that dark stretch of road, my mind was preoccupied with thoughts of my wife and children. And I believe because of that, I was allowed to reach a depth of love in that moment, which I would never have realized existed or understood otherwise. A depth of love that allowed me to release her from the hold of this world two and a half years later and has helped me to this day keep my life together, allowing me to be the father my children, even as adults, need me to be as I continually thank God for having allowed me to remain with them to share in the homecoming and the last few years of her life.

So, ask me about the power of love, and I'll tell you it's the most beautiful sensation, realization, or both that I know of. It's the peace I feel in those long, dark hours of the night when no breathing can be heard but that of my own as I remember the love we shared while peering across an empty pillow.

In closing, I like to say that what I had asked of God that night was nothing compared to the love that Christ must have had for all humanity to willingly give His life for all. As I realized the similarities that night between what I was requesting on my wife's behalf and what Christ had willingly done for me, it became infinitely clear to me just how much He must have loved me.

After all of this, I no longer have any issue with saying that I love ice cream or I love another individual or pet because I now know that love is so much more than we or our English language could ever begin to justify.

Our Love

It seems a lifetime ago in one sense,
and in another as if only yesterday, when we met.
Without our realizing it, we were both searching for someone special,
someone to share our lives with.
That's when God stepped in with a plan, joining our two hearts.
I know this because …
In a lifetime of years, I would never have thought of finding a love
such as yours and mine.
A love without sophistication or airs, just simple and enduring.
One where it wasn't you or me but us and we.
One that wasn't for convenience's sake
but just because we never wanted to be apart.
I remember well while courting
how we never wanted the night to end,
and when it did, it would hurt as though
we were never to see each other again;
and how we couldn't wait for the coming sunrise
and the new day to begin just so we could be together once again.
After we had married, and as the years passed,
we found ourselves right where we had started,
where we'd always been, never wanting it to end.

—M. L. Sutton

About M. L. Sutton

Mike Sutton, hailing from Flint, Michigan, and currently residing in Cheboygan on the sunrise side of Northern Michigan, presents an updated biography. A devoted father of two adult children living in the same region, Mike was married for 43 years until he sadly lost his wife to a health-related illness in May 2020.

In 2022, Mike embarked on his professional writing journey with the release of his debut book, *To Lose a Soul Mate,* published by Xulon Press. While the inspiration for this work stemmed from the loss of his wife, Mike believes he has been bestowed with a gift from God—a gift of expressing his heartfelt emotions and observations. This newfound talent allows him to perceive beauty amidst pain and grief, fostering gratitude and introducing him to new friendships.

Writing for pleasure, Mike shares his creations on social media platforms such as Writer's Café and Dirt Road Storytelling, and he is a featured contributor for BIZCATALYST 360. Additionally, Mike collaborates with like-minded authors in crafting impactful books.

The first was titled *Mission Hope, Thriving Through Seasons of the Soul,* a book featuring true stories of hope and rising above life's adversities. A book filled with encouragement and inspiration for those of us living in this constantly changing world. The second book, which is titled *Mission Hope, Volume II, Inspirational Stories of Faith and Triumph,* which became an Amazon best-selling book, shares their stories of faith and how it got them to where they are today; how it has helped them many times overcome insurmountable odds and live to tell others about it. And lastly, this book, *Mission Hope, Volume III,* which at the time of this writing is nearing its final stages of writing, deals with the power of love.

He doesn't know if blessings come in bundles, but he is once again thrilled to have been able to write with a group of wonderful writers, many of whom he's had the pleasure of writing with on past endeavors and new ones, while he awaits the printing of his second book, which is titled *For Him, For Her, For Them … An Anthology from the Heart.*

Prior to these life-changing events, he was enjoying retirement with his wife after having worked for 31 years with the State of Michigan Department of Natural Resources as a park manager in various parks throughout the state of Michigan. Today, his goal is to be the best parent that he can be and to help others who are struggling as he did and does after his wife's passing. Helping them to see that through God's love and the beauty that He has placed in our world, there is healing.

Power of Love

Babien Avila

I am by definition a "hopeless romantic." Always looking at the world through childlike eyes, rose-tinted glasses, music, and beauty. No situation, person, or thing could not be healed with a song. Even as a child, when I was disappointed or sad, just listening to and singing my favorite songs would soothe my soul and bring me back into a state of happiness. The songs that performed this magic were all about love. When I was around five years old, my parents gifted me with a transistor radio, noticing my interest in music. They added a record player a year or two later, which cemented my desire to be a singer and spread the love I felt so viscerally when I sang these songs. The harmonies set up a vibrational frequency that acted like serotonin for my soul. I still remember vividly being 10 and 11 years old and thinking about being happy dancing in a bubble of love with a future "soulmate," although I had not yet learned this terminology.

This romantic bubble eventually burst in my teen years, as my first experience with what I felt was soulmate love ran away after five months, lured by another. I have been carrying a bittersweet emotional undertone since, as love very often came with loss for me. My life has been punctuated by the highest ecstatic emotions as well as the lowest and darkest events. The more I sought contentment, the more it seemed to elude me. I longed for an even keel of peacefulness and smooth sailing, but those brief occurrences were rarely lasting. At times I wondered how others around me achieved this, yet my soul still craved the adrenaline rush of artistic performance, applause, and excitement while shying away from a more traditional path of stability. Romance, however, set me free like the excitement of the congas and the joys of salsa dancing. It felt so much like home. My path has been a journey of discovery led primarily by my heart.

Love truly is the answer and the driving force that creates all of life. I am a spiritual person with a core belief that my Higher Power, the God force within, guides our way and runs through our veins as love. Although the rose-colored glasses I viewed my world through as a child and young adult have dimmed somewhat due to some devastating losses, challenges, and lessons, this clarity has emerged anew with deep reflection. One truth I have always felt and still believe is that love is the essence of our Creator as well as the substance, or energy, we are created with. The vibrant and life-giving force of love is the creative principle made manifest through our thoughts, feelings, and dreams longing to be expressed with our children through music, dance, and art, as well as the manifestation of our goals and dreams. It still rings in my ears through music, whether I am listening, singing, or writing it. Love has given me strength and motivation when I lost my way and elevated my spiritual path, teaching me true happiness when I gave birth to my son Danilo and later my daughter Alexia.

After the premature loss of my first baby at 25.6 weeks, I lost a piece of my soul but not my determination to have another baby and a healthy pregnancy. Two months after that devastating event, I found out I was pregnant again to the dismay of my OB-GYN, who had cautioned against this for at least six months. God and the universe had another plan for me. I was ecstatic, of course, and this brought me out of the dark abyss of my private depression. It also brightened up my husband, Luis, and brought us both back to life.

I had just started a new job as a restaurant manager, which ended abruptly when my doctor placed me on bed rest at 22 weeks, declaring this pregnancy a high risk. This was due to my extremely late miscarriage several months earlier. I was not thrilled about this turn of events but felt committed to doing everything in my power to support a safe and healthy pregnancy for this new soul who chose me for their mother. My husband supported this decision wholeheartedly and told me to take it easy and rest. We decided to name the baby Danilo, after my husband's middle name, if it was a boy, or Alexia, after my grandfather Alex, if it was a girl.

I gradually felt better, healthier, and happier than I had felt in a long time. My cravings became quite bizarre; chicken livers and fried rice were a regular go-to. Yikes! I'm laughing here by the Hudson (River) recalling this memory and listening to "Roberta Flack" and "The Stones." It was difficult spending so much time alone when my husband was working, but I got productive, writing music and working on Astrology charts and spiritual readings for my clients. My wonderful father visited often and took me for walks along the Hudson near my apartment for exercise and enjoyment. This pregnancy was monitored very closely and, thankfully, was largely uneventful.

I gained a whopping 50 pounds and felt a bit awkward in this strange new body but took it all in stride. My primary goal was to give birth to a healthy full-term baby! Luis and I attended Lamaze classes and practiced deep breathing together in preparation for our baby boy's arrival, yet the due date came and went. I was encouraged to walk as much as possible; so, walk, I did all over the Upper West Side of Manhattan as well as at the hospital during my final checkups.

Ten days after my due date, I was admitted to the Hospital to start induction procedures and administered intravenous oxytocin to jump-start contractions. A baby cannot remain in the uterus after two weeks post-due date, yet my doctors ruled out a C-section, deciding on a natural birth. Baby Danilo was very content to remain inside and clearly in no rush to greet the world yet. Forty-eight hours later, I finally began getting strong contractions and started pushing. This continued for so long that I became exhausted. The nurse gave me oxygen and let me rest for a short time before moving forward with renewed pushing since I was almost fully dilated by that time. My OB then decided to do a suction delivery with a second physician because of the delay which could have become dangerous. Ultimately, forceps were required to pull Danilo out by the head! It was a protracted ordeal. This was 1995, and at the time, C-sections were not seen as the best option, but looking back, it probably would have been much less traumatic for both of us.

Baby Danilo seemed fine after they cleaned off the excess meconium caused by the late birth date and placed him on my chest. I cried with relief and exhaustion bonding with my newborn son until the nurses decided to take him for tests. I was encouraged to eat and rest to normalize my blood pressure, which was spiking up and down from this lengthy ordeal. When I woke up, I was told Danilo's breathing was extremely rapid, so he would have to remain in the NICU for a day or two to stabilize. This came as a shock that swept away any happiness I was feeling the day before and replaced it with worry. I was released from the hospital and told to go home with my husband and rest, that everything would be all right. This was hardly reassuring to us, the couple that had very recently lost a baby boy at 25.6 weeks.

Neither of us slept much that night. When we called the hospital in the morning, we were told that Danilo was in an incubator in the NICU where they were testing his blood, heart, and lungs, looking for any defects. We were able to see him later that day, and I started pumping breast milk daily at the hospital in their private breast pump rooms. They transferred my milk and fed Danilo in the incubator at regular intervals. I was worried I wouldn't be able to bond properly since I was not allowed to lift him from the incubator. This upset me greatly, so I asked to stay at the hospital near his incubator every day for 8-10 hours, and my husband would stay at night whenever possible. The nurses were wonderful and let me sing to him each day as we were feeding him and even afterward. I wrote a song for him, "Te Quiero Danilo" (I love you, Danilo), and sang it to him in Spanish and English. He would hear it and look at me. Sometimes he would smile. The nurses had to prick him with needles to take his blood, and I knew he must be in pain. It broke my heart that I could not pick him up to comfort him, so I sang instead and started feeding him my breast milk through a small bottle. This went on for 15 days.

Gradually Danilo's breathing became regulated, and the doctors talked about releasing him. They debated about sending equipment to our home to alert us in case he stopped breathing again, but eventually, it was decided he would sleep next to my bed in a bassinet. This way, I would be able to hear and check on him during the night. My husband and I took turns doing this for a year as I continued to sing "Te Quiero Danilo" as well as lullabies. We truly bonded in this way, and I was able to resume full breastfeeding for seven more months. This experience, as well as the tremendous loss we suffered with our first baby, taught me so much about the power of love and how it gives us the will and the strength to live as well as a purpose to go on.

Two years and four months later, I gave birth to a beautiful baby girl we named Alexia, and these two wonderful souls fill my heart with unending love and joy that just keeps increasing every year. They are now both healthy adults as well as my teachers and the only biological family I still have on this earth now. I know their father and my father, as well as my mother, in heaven are very proud. When we pass over, all we will take with us is the love we gave and received from others, as well as the beautiful self-love we hold within.

Writing these memories and documenting my personal history in this way brings a powerful surge of emotion and reminds me that my child-like vision of love was not so far off from the heart-centered way of life I choose to live now. Allowing my heart to speak first has brought some disappointments, yes, but the rewards of allowing love to flow through my being and inform my decisions keep me aligned and connected to my Divine source and purpose while allowing me to be my most authentic self through my work as a writer, speaker, teacher, or singer, and especially with my family and friends. Love, truly, is the answer.

Love is Light Above

The time has come to let our old fears fly
It doesn't help to dwell on pain, so let's not even try
The future is ours; the magic is here at last
My joy is growing stronger since I let go of the past
Love is light above
It's the thing we're most in need of
Love is light above
Rainbows of color will show us the dream of love, sweet love
The dance of life will show us all the way
To greater understanding if we just learn how to play
These makeshift lives we're living can't go on
The truth is ours to realize the vision's just begun
And when we turn away the darkness, light is all we see
The hope of love eternal sets us free
Love will save our lives
Love will save us—
Love

About Babien Avila

 Babien Avila is a best-selling author in *Mission Hope, Volume II*. She is a spiritual counselor and ordained minister, serves as a divine angel channel/healer, and is a published singer-songwriter. Her mission is to heal, uplift, and guide individuals facing crossroads in life, offering hope to those stuck in patterns or facing challenges.

Combining her spiritual gifts with music, she endeavors to create joy and meaning in others' lives through writing, speaking, singing, and private counseling. Blessed with clairaudience, clairsentience, and clairvoyance, Babien transitioned from a successful music career to focus on healing and spirituality, holding a BFA in theatre and music. Currently expanding her counseling work, she anticipates further contributions to the Mission Hope series while studying RTT therapy.

Love Translated

—

Mary Ann Falletta

In a world full of hate, there is love. How you translate it is ultimately up to you. I have experienced many different forms of love in my lifetime, all of which have taught me important life lessons, molded me into the woman I am today, and taught me the value of love.

I'm not even going to try to sugarcoat it … I was terrified to write this chapter. I have been putting off writing it for months now. I would start writing, write a page, and then walk away. I knew why I was having such a hard time, but I didn't want to admit it. All of those feelings—fears, emotions, remembering different circumstances—would absolutely make me cringe. It physically made my heart hurt; feeling that hurt would make me cry, and I absolutely hate to cry. I used to think that crying was a sign of weakness, but I learned that it's a sign of strength. Writing about love, or even the mere thought of love, terrifies me. My track record with love hasn't been the greatest, but it hasn't been the worst either. It's been somewhere in between, I suppose.

I had decided that I'm never getting married again. My whole philosophy on it was that when two people get married, one or both parties look at it as ownership. With that mentality, it's never going to work. After a while, people become complacent, take advantage of one another, take each other for granted, get bored, and the spark dies out, and the next thing you know, someone cheats. Then no one wants to divorce because of the cost and everything that can be lost. So, then, resentment builds up.

The way I looked at it was, I don't have to be married to be with someone for the rest of my life.

When you're not married, you know that the other person can leave anytime anything goes wrong. Therefore, you're more apt to try harder to please your significant other because you know they can walk with no strings attached at any given moment. So, you try harder; the spark doesn't die out; you don't take each other for granted; you don't take advantage of one another; and you respect each other more.

After years of healing, and let me just say that I'm still healing, I have come to the realization that each person is absolutely different and that not all people feel like a marriage is ownership. Not everyone enters into a marriage and takes each other for granted; that all depends on the person you attract and the kind of person you are. It has taken me years to come to this realization. I used to think that there was no one out there for me. After years of meditation, grounding, and growth, I learned something very important. That is, what you speak into the universe is what you get times10. For example, if I say I am worthy of love, and I am in a relationship, then that is exactly what I'm going to get—a loving relationship. This goes back to "Be careful what you say because words are powerful." Have you ever realized that when you say negative things, negative events happen? When you say positive things, then positive things are going to happen; then they do happen. This is not a coincidence. I live by this mantra, and it has been life-changing.

As I started preparing to write this chapter again this morning, I stood in my kitchen and thought to myself, *OK, I can either continue to dread writing this chapter, or I can use this chapter to help me and help you, my readers, heal.* In that moment, I had so many different feelings, emotions, and fears running through my mind. However, I decided to let it heal me first. So, I stood in my kitchen and said out loud, "Lord, I need you to use me as a vessel; let the words just flow through me effortlessly, powerfully, and without fear. Please, allow me the opportunity to heal my heart, my mind, and my soul; and most importantly, God, please allow the words in my chapter help others to heal emotionally, physically, mentally, and as painlessly as possible." I then translated my prayer of love into: "I am going to heal my heart, my mind, emotionally, physically, and mentally. I will find love, peace, joy, happiness, abundance in love, and financial abundance." As I was saying my "I am" statements, it felt like electricity rapidly running through my body, from my head to my toes and all the way back up to my head and back through my toes over and over again. It felt comforting, safe, victorious, and freeing. As the tears were flowing freely, I could feel the transformation of healing. This, my friends, is the power of not only God and love but manifestation.

Have you ever sat and thought to yourself, *What is love*? Like, *What does love really mean?* Lord knows I have. I can't tell you the countless times that I have cried myself to sleep or just taken a moment to sit down or stand up somewhere or even drive down the road, listening to a song on my playlist and just crying it out. It is so healing. I think of it as cleansing all the hurt, negativity, and toxicity out of my body, mind, and soul. It is empowering and freeing.

There are multiple definitions for love; one is: an intense feeling of deep affection. As a noun, it means a great interest or pleasure in something. As a verb, it means feeling deep affection for someone. However, the Old English origin of the word love means desires or pleasing. So, why does love hurt so much if it's supposed to be pleasing? Let me translate my personal answer to that question for you: it's not the love that is hurting you; it's the choice or choices you make and how you allow your circumstances to affect you. I can't tell you how many times I blamed love for the hurt that I was feeling before realizing that it was not love or the lack of love that was causing the hurt but the way that I allowed my circumstances to affect me.

I haven't been in a long-lasting relationship since my divorce in 2018. The longest committed relationship that I've had is one month. Just 30 days; that's it! The reason I haven't is that the expectations that I originally set for how a man was supposed to love me were unrealistic and unobtainable. For example, I literally thought that if a man didn't text me back within a few minutes, he didn't want anything to do with me, and I would just tell him that I was done with him. It was just unacceptable for me. What I didn't realize is, it's also unacceptable for them as well. What I didn't take into account is that they have lives—jobs, family, etc. I was being completely irrational. Even worse is that I didn't realize this until almost two years ago, and I had put myself in a mental prison. I was constantly fighting for my worthiness all because I had set unreasonable expectations.

We've all had feelings of deep affection for many things, right? We've all had a great interest or pleasure in something at some point in our lives, but how do those feelings make you feel, though? Those feelings you feel in your soul or gut are just a couple of ways that you are experiencing the power of love. Love is so universal, yet so misunderstood. It's so complex, yet so simple.

You can have relationships where someone is a soulmate or an exact mirror of yourself. In fact, we have several different soulmates; they can be male or female. I personally have several soulmates in my life, both males and females. My soulmates are a mere reflection of myself. We understand each other so deeply and are so connected that we can feel what one another is going through. I know this sounds bizarre, but it is a fact.

I have several men in my life, and I love each one of them in a different way. Two of them being my son and my son-in-law. There are multiple examples that I can give, but that's not the important thing here, is it? How they make me feel is not only important but also detrimental. I have different feelings for them and for different reasons. Some make me feel like the best version of myself, like I can take on the world, and I'm successful; some make me feel powerful, safe, loved, supported, and respected; and some just make me feel. In Greek Mythology, the love that I have for some translates to Eros and Agapic love. Eros love is, and I quote, "not only passionate in a sexual or spiritual nature but amazingly beautiful and desirable," whereas Agapic love is, and I quote, "a love that is manifested when one has much to give to another more needy without expecting anything in return." I have certain relationships that are categorized as Philia love, which is, and I quote, "friends with mutual compatibility and common values."

I have some of the absolute best friends in the entire world, and I don't say that lightly either. They are funny, smart, straightforward, compassionate, and sweet, yet protective of me and loyal. They have been there for me when I've been at my worst and my best. What I absolutely love about them is that they have the ability to be genuine and bold; they put me in my place (in a loving way, of course) when I am wrong; they support me when I need it. They have helped me to grow by leaps and bounds and have never once judged me. I consider them my sisters, not by blood but by heart. They are my balance, my soulmate, and my sounding board, and for all of this, I am extremely grateful and humbled.

I will never forget the first time I ever experienced love. It was a deep feeling of comfort, safety, compassion, respect, and satisfaction, knowing that no matter what, I would always be loved by someone in this world unconditionally. The first time that I ever experienced love was the love that I had for my mother and the love that she showed me every single day. I can remember as far back as the age of five or six, I had taken off down the road to go visit my friend to play with her without telling my mother, and I was unattended. My mom got in her car, yelling my name, Mary Ann Elizabeth, out of her car window as she slowly drove down the road. We all know that when our parents called us by first and middle name, we were in serious trouble. I was so scared; my heart was racing. I could hear her car getting closer and closer. I had nowhere to run. Then she found me. I just knew I was safe long enough for her to get me home before I got a spanking. Nope, she did it right there in my friend's driveway. I remember being so embarrassed but so hurt because she spanked me in front of my friend. I knew that I had let her down. I remember, to this day, every time my mother would spank me, she would say, "I'm doing this because I love you." As I got older, I became quite sarcastic, and of course, the spankings were more frequent. Now let me set the record straight: my mom never beat me; she disciplined me with love. There's a difference.

My mother was not only an amazing mom but an amazing woman. She dedicated her whole life to raising her children. She would take me shopping, to the movies, bingo, the swimming pool … really, anywhere I wanted to go. What I remember the most about my mom is her love for me. She always made sure to tell me every single night before bed that she loved me. I knew that she did because I could feel her love and compassion when she would say it. It made me feel safe, loved, worthy, and like I was enough just as I am. The love that she showed me taught me how to love, how to be loved, and how to express love. It also taught me a lot of life lessons. What it didn't teach me was how to handle heartbreak.

The heartbreak I am referring to is my mother's passing away. My siblings and I knew it was coming, so we each mentally prepared for it. Let me say this: I don't care how much you prepare for the death of your mother; you're never fully prepared. My mother was the glue that held our family together. She was the love that made you feel accepted, like nothing you did was ever wrong if you put your heart into it. She was the voice of reason, my moral compass, my best friend, the person who everyone went to for advice, and if you didn't want to hear the truth, then don't ask for her opinion because she's going to give it to you straight, whether you like it or not. I know that my mother is watching me from heaven, and I can only hope that I am at least half the woman she was. Never, ever take your mother's love for granted. Spend every waking moment you can with her. Let her tell her stories over and over because I assure you, there's something you need, and there's a lesson in it. Treasure those moments so you don't find yourself later wishing you had.

As I got older and became a mom myself, I learned to appreciate the lessons that my mother taught me and started seeing what she meant by "I'm doing this because I love you." All of sudden, that aha moment happened.

At the age of 22, I had my first child. I wasn't married because I chose not to be. The father of my child had some habits that I didn't approve of, so I opted out. I was raised as an Italian Catholic, so having a baby out of wedlock was not exactly kosher, and my family knew, as well as myself, that I wasn't ready to be a mother. But the moment that I felt my son kick inside of me, I fell in love and knew that I needed to change. I had him two days before Christmas, and that was the best Christmas gift ever. I don't know how to explain the love that I had for him. I felt whole, complete, and most importantly protective and scared—all at the same time. Shortly, after having him, I met a man that I later married. That, right there, was a completely different kind of love. I felt secure and loved for a little while. Then I became pregnant and delivered my daughter exactly one week before my birthday. She was the best birthday present anyone could ask for. Again, as soon as I felt her kick inside of me, I instantly fell in love, and the first time that I looked into both of my children's eyes and held them close, I knew that no other love could ever replace that kind of love. I knew that without a doubt, my children were the only people in the world who would love me forever, unconditionally, and that I would love them and protect them, no matter what the cost was.

My children are my life; they are what has kept me and still keep me going to this day. I would walk through fire for them if it meant saving their lives, just like any mother would. I am now a grandparent, and I go by Mimi. I have two grandchildren who were born a little over a week ago and four days apart (as of the time of this writing), now giving me a total of six grandchildren, and now, a new kind of love has been born. A love that is unconditionally connected to me and my children. My grandchildren are an extension of their parents, of that unconditional love that I have set aside in my heart and soul. This, my friends, is love translated into the perception of myself, my life experiences, and what love means to me.

Thank you for the opportunity to share with you. I would like to leave you with one last thing: Love does not have to be complicated. It just needs to be kind, patient, supportive, equal, loyal, trusting, and most importantly emotionally healthy. Set boundaries for yourself and others but also make sure that not only do you support your own boundaries but theirs as well.

Lastly, but certainly not least, if you have been through some traumatic experiences or experienced hurt from a past relationship, heal those traumas first before entering into another relationship. If you don't, you will end up taking those past relationship traumas into your next relationship. That's not fair to them or yourself. Love yourself first. It starts with you. You can't love someone else if you don't love yourself. I wish you love, light, and healing.

About Mary Ann Falletta

 Mary Ann, a mother, grandmother, sister, aunt, and friend, is a best-selling author in *Mission Hope, Volume II.* With roots in Monroe, Louisiana, and raised in an Italian Catholic family, she developed independence from her nurse mother, who single-handedly raised three children. Mary Ann learned Italian by eavesdropping on her mother and grandmother's conversations.

Having spent her entire school life in a private Catholic institution, referred to humorously as "Prison and Plaid," Mary Ann transitioned to college at NLU (now ULM) in Monroe, Louisiana, and later pursued further education at ASU Beebe in Arkansas.

Post-college, Mary Ann secured a promotion in her current job, leading her to relocate to Cabot, Arkansas, with her children. Obtaining certifications as a domestic violence counselor and advocate, she initiated domestic violence support groups; collaborated with local law enforcement; and, with the support of state officials, including a state senator and representative, authored the "No Drop Law." This law, now adopted by 39 states, ensures that if a victim drops charges, the state intervenes to prosecute the abuser.

Beyond her advocacy, Mary Ann identifies as a clairvoyant and empath deeply attuned to others' emotions. Her fervent hope is that individuals, even if just one, will find the strength to stand up for their beliefs, recognize their worth, and understand the transformative power of saying NO to abuse.

Footprints In Heaven

Elizabeth R. Urabe

This is Love:
To fly towards a secret sky
To cause a hundred veils to fall each moment.

First, to let go of life;
Finally ... to take a step without feet.

—Rumi

Those who know me at all know that I have a strong aversion to borrowing words from other people, especially well-known individuals whose quotes are often used simply to draw attention to the work of those whose self-confidence and realization don't yet allow for the conviction-based expression of personal truth and experience. But I have actually had the wisdom of my poetry compared to that of Rumi just as I have been included as a favorite abstract artist in such sublime company as Picasso and Salvador Dali. So, I have chosen to start my chapter in *Mission Hope, Volume III,* with this less-known but particularly powerful and accurate description by the master of profound poetry in the hopes that I will be successful in springboarding off the living energies with which it infuses me and be able to put into language that which is essentially inexpressible: love and how love has been a guiding light on my journey through time and space, homeward bound toward conscious reunion with eternity once again.

Initially, I had decided that it wasn't written in the stars for me to be one of the co-authors in *Volume III* of the Mission Hope anthology! I was supremely happy with the chapter downloaded for *Volume II*, and despite several months of intense contemplation of multiple possibilities for stories from the archives of my passionately fascinating life story, I just wasn't feeling that there was anything right now wanting to be born through me. And if there's one lesson I've learned over the decades and learned well, it's that true creativity cannot be forced. When a fruit is ripe, it falls naturally from the tree, or so spoke a wise mango in organic response to a cry for help and understanding that I made early one morning in the garden of the mother ashram of my yogic lineage in Maharashtra, India, back in 1998. But I digress.

To get back to love, when I told Mission Hope inspiration and orchestrator Char Murphy that I just wasn't "feeling it" to be in *Volume III*, she was disappointed and seemed to accept my decision for a minute or two, at least. But Char is like a Pitt Bull; once she gets her mind convinced that something is destined to happen, there ain't no way on God's green earth that she's going to let it go. So, she kept dropping hints, none of them particularly subtle, but all of them respectful. That's one of the key ingredients of genuine love; respect for the fact that each and every person has the divine right to see things differently and arrive at what is true for them in his or her own timing. I knew that Char had 19 of the 20 authors that she wanted for book III and that she was still hoping that I would have a change of heart and agree to write a chapter. But as I said, creativity cannot be forced, and while I could have succumbed to my baser instincts and gotten pissed off at her relentless pursuit, I love Char as a soul and spirit sister, and so I trusted her process as much as I do my own and kept lovingly but respectfully declining.

Then, only yesterday, late in the afternoon, she reached out and asked if I would consider submitting one of my many poems that had love at the core to be in the book because she has great appreciation for the power of my poetry. I figured she was thinking of having my words be the poetic introduction to *Mission Hope, Volume III,* and I immediately and enthusiastically agreed. Char waited an appropriate moment or two before suggesting that maybe multiple poems might be well received. My response was, "Hell yeah! The more, the merrier!" Another pregnant pause, like a hawk watching its prey, before she went for the jugular: "While you›re at it, it would make sense to have a connecting sentence or two between poems so there›s artistic integrity to the body of work."

Well, that, too, sounded completely agreeable and doable to me, and then I immediately laughed at how she had cleverly gotten me to agree to write what would end up being a chapter in the book, albeit in mostly poetry form. It›s not easy to "pull one over" on "Grandma Beth," as I am often called, but Char is one of the few and rare individuals capable of "out grandma-ing" me.

So, when I went to bed last night, my idea was to compile a nice selection of poetry, write a handful of sentences about love, and send it all to Char to let her put the pieces together the way her heart and spirit felt them. But apparently, the universe had other plans because the Rumi quote, one of my favorites, was running through my head when I got up in the morning, and I had the distinctly sneaky suspicion that I was going to end up—in joyous surrender—writing a full chapter after all, with poems scattered here and there in multidimensional creative support of the prose.

Poem #1

Natural disasters send
and paradoxically portend
Spiritual dividend
divine gifts right around the end

Our Mother Earth is on the mend
as from the heavens gods descend
Here our ancient wounds to tend
and help us from old forms ascend

To new dimensions that depend

on Truth alone and don't pretend
In times of need a hand to lend
support as unknown ways we wend

With fear and doubt we must contend
but never choose our Souls to vend
For pennies, power, pleasure's trend
sentence of a life condemned

Intuition to befriend
things the mind can›t comprehend
Great energy must we extend
and man-made villains apprehend

Outdated judgments we suspend
seeking to our pain amend
With healing stories freshly penned
no longer striving to offend

So let our prayers for peace extend
and every waking moment spend
Focused on the nightmare›s end …
and effort, everywhere commend.

—E.R. Urabe (February 2022)

Love is the glue that holds the integrity of the universe intact, even when human beings are completely ignorant or egotistically uncaring about universal law. Love is God›s promise to each and every one of us that, no matter how horrific our actions may have been in time, the eternal purity at the core of our being remains innocent and untouched. Love is the energetic presence that gives us the strength to do and be certain ways in situations where survival instincts of fight or flight are screaming to be followed. I was in a long-term relationship for many years with a man who carried wounds from childhood trauma that he had never been ready or willing to face, feel, and allow to be healed. I knew in my gut that the day would come when life would force him to stop running away from himself, but I had no idea what form that wake-up call would take.

We had a long run of years where we brought out the best in each other, co-created an incredible legacy, and grew tremendously as individuals. But the day came when everything inevitably began to unravel, and the pain he had been carrying around for more than half a century began to rear its ugly head directed often violently toward me because I believe that, subconsciously, he knew that I was the only person strong enough to bear witness and not crumble under the weight of his suffering.

There were days where literally he would be pouring out verbal and sometimes physical abuse for as much as 15 hours straight, and I would have to beg to be allowed to take a pee break. Because faith and surrender have been pillars of the foundation of my path in the world, although I was brought to my knees in exhaustion each and every time, I was somehow able to open to the energy of the situation, never losing the conscious awareness of consciousness, which is, to me, grace; the power that ultimately heals all wounds. I didn›t try to pacify or argue with him because I knew that to do so would only add fuel to the fire. I simply accepted. Accepted the expression of his pain as it emerged; accepted the struggle it was for me to remain centered through each storm. Accepted the inner knowing that there was healing yet to be received within myself and that, in God›s timing, all would be revealed.

Poem #2

In the place of Truth abide
where all are One with no divide
In the place of peace reside
where joy is always amplified

In the place of trust confide
where black and white live side by side
Where suffering no more can hide
the fact of Unity belied

Responsibility denied
equates to guilt or blame implied
But neither one can change the tide
of fear projected, seen outside

We called for help and God replied
each dualistic knot untied
All hidden masks identified
endless grace, support supplied

So find your pace, maintain your stride
let not the ego faith deride
No chance to waste or time to bide
on fabled Pegasus astride

And from this silent space decide
that Consciousness will be your guide
Not husband, status, wealth or pride
but true compassion, your sole guide

Let freedom's bell ring far and wide
that no heart locked be left untried
Set all differences aside
and find the sameness deep inside

That love might hatred override
assimilated and applied
With no illusion undecried …
Truth reigns unquestioned, undefied.

—E.R. Urabe (May 2022)

It has taken me 10 years to truly understand and assimilate the fact that I had multiple unconscious wounds of my own that he was reflecting back to me. Projection makes perception. I wasn›t ready at the time to face, feel, and heal my own emotional scars, but because I am a true warrior of the Spirit, I have been able to trace my way back to every single incident that happened between us and recognize that I played a pivotal role in all of it. And today, our relationship—while different in form—is rooted in a degree of honest love, friendship, and respect for who we are now precisely because of everything we went through together during the stormy periods.

But even while we were still together, one experience comes to mind about the power of love to shine through any clouds. We had gone to an art show to showcase a large selection of my work at the Mandalay Bay resort in Las Vegas, quite a change from the remote mountaintop home in the middle of nowhere that we called home. We were both nervous and anxious in the foreign setting and circumstances, and instead of being of emotional support to one another, we fussed, got angry, and picked at each other critically, but we managed to pull ourselves together and get through the three days with a decent amount of balance and composure. When the show was over, we were packing everything up and just getting ready to head back to Arizona when a woman approached us. Exultantly, she exclaimed, "I've been looking all over for you two!"

Somewhat confused, we asked and waited for clarification. She explained that she had seen us together the morning of our arrival working to unload our Honda Odyssey and get all of the artwork onto a dolly for transport into the hotel for the show. Then she said that she had never seen or witnessed such profound love between two people in her entire life, and she was so moved by what she felt that she'd spent three entire days tracking us down to share this with us. The exchanges that I had judged as being nothing more than childish arguing were, in her eyes, a flow of love and deep, unconditional caring. It was an inexpressibly humbling experience for me and one which I never forgot, one that would serve me well later in life as well.

Poem #3

Surrender to God's Will despite
the pressure to conform and fight

The time has come not to indict
but to unravel and rewrite

Each tale of suffering and plight
must choose through Grace to reignite
A vision joyous, pure and white
with healing for all within sight

And when fear beckons in the night
dispel it with your inner light
Strong enough all wrongs to right
as angels witness with delight

When on the ground seek not the height
the eagle reaches when in flight
But rather, patiently, sit tight
and thus true miracles invite

To bless your life with gentle might
ancient wisdom to excite
Emerging messengers alight …
and a new story do indite.

—*E.R. Urabe (October 2021)*

How easily we judge and condemn others for their uncontrolled actions when, in truth, our own thoughts are full of guilt and blame, the twin triggers of all violence! It seems easier to project our own unacknowledged pain onto someone "out there" rather than meeting it within ourselves and taking responsibility within and without for the conditions of our lives and our world. There›s a little bit of Hitler in everyone. To deny that truth is precisely why we create monsters in history; they are the attempt to wake us up to our own hypocrisy and unconscious bias.

To heal means to make whole. Love takes seemingly separate entities or opposing thoughts, positions, opinions, and experiences and energetically brings us back to the ultimate truth that there›s only one of us. Each and every person on the planet, no matter how flawed or wounded, is a precious, priceless, integral part of the one Self that we share. Infinite waves in an endless ocean of consciousness fighting with each other about differences of size or intensity. A tidal wave is made of the same stuff as a single drop of water. In form and purpose, they are completely different. In essence, they are identical. Love demands that we not only intellectually grasp this concept but embody it. Fully and completely. With every thought, word, and action. Consciously. Until we achieve this state, we are only paying lip service to using the word love in a society where people love their spouse and love pizza in the same breath and heartbeat.

Love is unconditional. We must make peace with the paradox of polarity and opposites, all of which are vitally important tools for growth as we awaken and progress. Most people are running away from one form in search of another form that they think will give them permanent and lasting joy. This is nothing more than the fickleness of ego. The moment you achieve a goal born of ego, you realize it hasn›t satisfied you. Die to each moment that life might live through you, free and unencumbered. This is love.

Poem #4

Will it be good news or will it be bad?
I know not the difference for that I am glad
The Conductor of Truth holds our life in His hand
Minds cannot grasp but our hearts understand

This isn›t a game, not a trend nor a fad
but the climax of lifetimes with nothing to add
Alone before God stripped of fear do we stand
in places and spaces where once we felt banned

With steadfast devotion no leaning to gad
to stray from our course or waste time being sad
Homeward bound toward a new and proclaimed promised land

Souls united as One to an ancient comman

In feathers of freedom our forms now are clad
released from the shackles of pain we once had
Committed to destiny, not what we planned ...
Surrendered to grace, flame by flame strand by strand.
—E. R. Urabe (December 2022)

What I have discovered in the past year is that it is the emotional body that is in most need of healing attention. We have not one but four bodies: physical, emotional, mental, and spiritual. I have seen that people who are successful by eternal standards—good-looking, intelligent, and capable—are the ones who get away with not addressing their core emotional wounds for the longest time. I know because I was one of them. But eventually, all masks must be stripped away, or, as Rumi says, we must cause a hundred veils to fall each moment, if we are to reconnect to the Truth of our being and attain the highest possible state here on planet Earth so as to truly be of service. What is required is the willingness to burn in the fire of grace; to feel every uncomfortable, painful, or unbalanced emotion fully and completely, without judgment, and without trying to run away or put new bandaids on old boo-boos. We are brought to our knees time and time again in such humility that our entire being cries out to God to end our suffering. We feel like we can›t go on. And yet, somehow, something deep, deep inside us knows that we aren›t really dying but being reborn. And we muster all the hope and faith we›re capable of and allow the multifaceted aspects of love to hurt as much as they bring pleasure and joy until one day, finally, blessedly, we wake up and realize that the sun is shining. Literally and figuratively. The nightmare is over. And a new earth has been born through us.

Tears of gratitude are streaming from my heart now as I prepare to end this unplanned, love-inspired chapter with one of my personal favorite rhyming poems titled "Nightmare's End." Both Char and I played our divine roles perfectly in our dance of push and shove, hope and faith, trust and surrender, culminating in this love-filled offering that has poured out of me in a matter of just a couple of hours. I will leave you with this thought, again borrowed from the beloved poet Rumi's quote with which I began this sacred writing, "If you have gotten this far, you have already let go of life. Now it is time to take a step without feet."

Poem #5

I released my guilt today
and blessedly, it flew away
No longer trapped in liar›s lair
I freely soar from here to there

And back again into the fray
of warring minds, the ego›s prey
Armed now with joy beyond compare
I scatter light rays everywhere

Like the Sun at break of day
dispelling darkness come what may
Accepting every cosmic dare
of disbelief and faithless fare

Planting seeds of peace I pray
that all might feast and find their way
Through illusion›s blinding glare
and of their bounty gladly share

With their brothers, fear at bay
no longer under selfish sway
With generosity to spare
nothing is too much to bear

I released all guilt today
and blessedly, it flew away
On wings of Grace, now light as air …
of Truth alone I am aware.

—E. R. Urabe (June 2022)

About Elizabeth R. Urabe

As an artist, Elizabeth R. Urabe has always had only one goal: to translate the invisible energies of Absolute Truth into tangible form using abstract design, color, poetic imagery, and prose so that an ever-increasing number of people might have a more direct access to the inner realms of human existence.

In early 1995, Elizabeth spontaneously began to draw the pictures now known as Urabe Spirit Art and, to date, has channeled more than 750 designs. No thought is ever involved in the birthing process, and she has always referred to her role as that of a "spiritual midwife" rather than the creator of this extraordinary body of work. Remarkably, despite the incredible complexity of design and detail, no single picture has ever taken longer than one week to complete.

In 2011, Elizabeth was one of three first-place winners of the American Batik Design Competition organized by (then) the ambassador to the US from the Indonesian embassy in Washington D.C., Dr. Dino Patti Djalal, with her powerful design Divine Unity. As a result, she was awarded a three-week tour of some of the most prominent batik and fashion companies in Indonesia and now has contacts in Jakarta who have created breathtakingly beautiful silk shawls for ladies and one-of-a-kind original shirts for men, each piece endowed with the living 4000-year-old history of Indonesia's perfected batik techniques and the essence of Urabe Spirit Art as both the energetic and design inspiration.

Most recently, Elizabeth has launched a website of several hundred diverse products, each one empowered to assist in the spiritual processes of awakening, healing, and reintegration and transformation of old karmic impressions. This is the first time that the unparalleled energies of Urabe Spirit Art have been made easily accessible on a global scale, but this is only the tip of the iceberg. As worn-out social structures continue to crumble, Urabe will be a leading presence guiding humanity toward the creation of a new earth.

In Elizabeth's words, "Urabe Spirit Art, in whatever myriad forms it may take, is one of the most powerful reflections of source energies available to us at this point in the evolution of consciousness. We are at a crossroads where the fate of our planet and life as we know it may very well depend on the willingness of each individual to embrace the entire spectrum of human emotion and commit to the kind of transformation that only real spiritual growth can offer. There is no longer any middle ground, and as long as we (still) believe that love has an opposite, we are (still) living in fear."

It is time for us to say an unequivocal yes to destiny and to take our rightful places as warriors of the Spirit. Let us join in this pure and noble vision, knowing that together, there is nothing we cannot accomplish.

Websites: www.urabeofficial.com
www.artstudioprints.com/elizabeth-urabe
www.erurabe.com
www.artstudioprints.com/elizabeth-urabe

Love Has the Power to Heal

——

Jennifer Bassett Beard

Moons and Junes and Ferris Wheels
The dizzy dancing way that you feel
As every fairy tale comes real
I've looked at love that way

But now it's just another show
And you leave 'em laughing when you go
And if you care, don't let them know
Don't give yourself away

I've looked at love from both sides now
From give and take and still somehow
It's love's illusions that I recall
I really don't know love
Really don't know love at all.

—Joni Mitchell (song: "Both Sides Now")

I think many of us would agree that love hurts and is experienced and expressed in different ways. If you had asked me 10 years ago how I feel about the topic of romantic love, I would have quoted the famous title of a song by the J. Geils Band, "Love Stinks."

I do think, however, that love gets a bad rap because it's blamed for people who have been hurt hurting other people and for so many unrealistic expectations. I have been on both the receiving and giving end of this pain train. I am no expert on love nor do I claim to be. I am simply sharing my experiences with love and how I allowed love to heal me.

What helped me heal and identify what love is, I began by defining what love is not. Here are the three things I identified that love isn't:

- Love isn't abusive
- Love isn't conditional
- Love isn't addiction

For the purpose of this chapter, I will focus on the first thing I found that love isn't—love isn't abusive.

Love Isn't Abusive

No one deserves to be abused. It's not love; it is a hurt individual either unconsciously or consciously sharing the pain they have never healed from. Yes, I think they should be held accountable for their actions. But I also think the only way people can heal is to identify why they are abusive and then try and break the cycle. For example, my ex-husband was sentenced to 28 years in prison, with 10 years suspended, for what he did to my daughters. He served 12 years and got out early for good behavior. He had attempted two other times to get released early before he was finally granted permission. My daughters and I were allowed to participate in the review process and express whether we agreed with him being released. Both times, it was found that he had not received any counseling for pedophilia. The judge thankfully denied his earlier requests, but he got out after 12 years, and it was never clear if he ever received any treatment. What is really concerning to me is that I recently found out that he has remarried a woman with a young daughter. He claimed he was "saved" in prison, and I pray he got the help he needed before being released. Having experienced the anguish of being a mother to children who were sexually abused, I wouldn't wish it on my worst enemy.

I suffered abuse at the hands of my ex-husband. He was very controlling and had a severe, unpredictable temper. He could go from 1–100 in an instant, and it was unpredictable what would set him off. The kids would beat him at a game and tease him about losing, and he would lose his cool. Other times, he would tease them back. It was very confusing for the kids as well. He physically abused me early on in the relationship until I fought back and told him I would leave. I would intervene when he would lose his cool and yell at the children. I thought I was protecting them but then came to find out he was sexually abusing my oldest daughter. He underestimated the strength of these young women because my second oldest daughter spoke up. I'm so proud of all of my daughters for speaking out.

When I was a child, my older sister was sexually abused by a relative, and when we tried to speak up, we were told that we were lying. It wasn't until years later that it came out that this relative had abused not only my sister but our cousin as well. This was after years of my sister trying to escape the shame and anger she felt inside with drugs and self-destructive behaviors. The wonderful news is that she has healed and has found love.

My ex and I spent our entire relationship in and out of counseling. He would do good for a while and then have a relapse. I was committed to making this marriage work because I had already had one divorce and saw firsthand how this impacted my three daughters from my first marriage. I caused pain to my children unconsciously because I had not healed from my own trauma growing up, which is a topic for another chapter or book.

I'm not sure if my ex was bipolar or not, but his attorney tried to use both the bipolar and brain tumor defense when trying to get his sentence reduced. He was diagnosed with brain cancer shortly after our first son was born, and I was reassigned from Mountain Home Air Force Base (AFB), Idaho, to Elmendorf AFB, Alaska. What I do know is that this man hurt the most valuable things in my life, and that's when I realized that I could not and would not stand for this. Not only would I not stand for it, but also, I was going to prosecute him to the fullest extent of the law. This was not a popular stance with some of the religious leaders in the Mormon Church. It was weird. My bishop in Alaska was all for my plan of action and supported me, but a few of the bishops in Utah were not impressed with my choice. In my mind, I felt that regardless of the relationship to the child, pedophilia is wrong, and people who practice it should be punished. It will be up to God to judge and decide their fate in the next life, but here, I had a chance to get justice for my daughters, and so I went for it! The district attorney of Alaska was gung-ho and told me once that she wished more mothers would prosecute their husbands for this. The majority of cases she had dealt with, the mothers chose to believe their significant other. I could still remember what it had felt like being told that my sister and I were lying about our step-grandpa abusing her. I couldn't do that to my daughters.

I truly loved my ex-husband and had fought hard for our marriage, so the betrayal I felt was beyond any pain I had ever experienced. I could have handled an affair but not the rape of my daughters. You can imagine the feelings that were brought up from my past with my sister's abuse and my own experiences with sexual abuse. My first thought was to hurt him; we had guns in the house, and I knew how to shoot them. But reason came to me quickly, thank God, because I had six children to care for, and I would be no good to them in prison. My next response was what I had done all my life when things got rough. I would not deal with the emotions, compartmentalizing them for later, when I had time to deal with them. The problem was that the time never came to deal with them until I was 48 years old, and I think God decided that the only way to help this crazy woman was to actually stop her. I'm just kidding, of course, but it feels that way.

It was time to pull up my big girl pants because I had six children aged 1–16 to care for. I had to sell my beautiful home in Eagle River, Alaska, and prepare to move my family to Salt Lake City, Utah, because I wanted to be closer to my family. It was so hard to leave Alaska because of the amazing friends I had and the amazing Eagle River community we were a part of. I will forever be thankful to those who showed me and my family love and refused to judge. These were true Christian people who actually helped me get my home ready to sell and prepared countless meals for my family. When we left, some of these people gave us a box full of coupons to eat at different restaurants while we were getting settled. It was a humbling, humiliating, painful, and difficult experience, but it taught me that love is serving one another. When someone is down on their luck, we can judge them, or we can reach out and see how we can help them. The Master of showing love and compassion helped the lame man walk, raised Lazarus from the dead, healed the blind, and cured the woman with a blood disorder. He forgave the woman taken in adultery and washed the feet of his apostles.

Through this whole experience as a nurse and mother, I took care of everyone else, except myself, and my hurt turned to anger and bitterness. I became a woman I didn't recognize. When we suffer a traumatic event in our lives and are really hurt, and we don't take the time to heal, it messes us up inside. At least it did for me. We begin to behave in ways and do things we wouldn't normally do just to feel some temporary relief from the hurt … the deep ache … the incessant pain.

I was also scared to death! I never planned to have such a big family, and certainly, not alone. We got involved in the Mormon church, and family is a strong part of this religion. My ex-husband had never been married and wanted children, so we decided to have two kids together, which made five, and an awesome sixth surprise was my 10 lb. baby boy.

Fast forward 12 years ago when I was diagnosed with multiple sclerosis. I pushed myself the way I always do, thinking that it was not going to slow me down. I was a homecare manager for Intermountain Homecare, Salt Lake City Branch. This was one of the most difficult experiences of my life—to watch my cognitive ability to manage my homecare team slip away. I loved my team; I had academic plans for the future to become a nurse practitioner. Now, I could barely walk a few steps before fatigue set in. I had brain fog so severe I couldn't drive or perform complex cognitive tasks. My vision was wonky, and I actually began slurring my speech in a work meeting. Yeah, it was both scary and humiliating.

I hit the lowest part of my life to the point where I thought seriously about checking out. I think I was still a little angry with God. Losing my career was like losing my lifeline. It was the thing I threw myself into in order to avoid dealing with the volumes of boxed-up emotions stored on the shelves of my heart and mind, waiting to be dealt with. Now I was faced with healing my entire being—my body, mind, and soul. All the scary, painful feelings that had been securely tucked away were erupting within me.

Fast forward, I didn't give up. I dug in and began healing myself through learning to love myself again. I did an amazing exercise—by Gabby Bernstein—where I reached my inner child and embraced her. This sounded weird to me at first, but I was open to healing, so I tried it, and it turned out to be one of the coolest experiences of my life. I saw myself standing in the hallway of my aunt's house (the aunt who raised me as a child). I was wearing the blue dress I had worn in a professional photo of my sister and me when we were five and three, and I could actually see the blue fish barrette in my curly pigtails. I felt so much compassion for this little girl who basically at age two lost her mom, dad, brothers, and sisters. She didn't understand what happened to them or why because she was just a child. I felt so much love for her. I hugged her tightly, and while I was hugging her, all the self-hate, guilt, unworthiness, and shame I was carrying inside melted away for that moment in time. These self-limiting beliefs and emotions would later return for me to address, but this experience allowed me to feel for a moment what it was like to release these heavy, toxic beliefs and feelings that I had carried around for so long, and I wanted to feel that release permanently.

This was the beginning of my healing journey. I even started a Facebook page titled "Finding My Balance in an Upside-Down World," where I have shared insights from my journey. My followers help inspire me. I began with a full-on approach. I know that our minds and bodies are connected, so I knew I had to heal my physical health, along with my mental health, in order to truly heal. I didn't want any more anti-anxiety drugs or anti-depressants. That was always the answer when I would go to the doctor. I wanted to be able to feel my life. I had tried the drugs they recommended, and they just made me feel like I was a robot. My goal was to wean off of them.

The most important thing I did to begin healing was to learn how to love and forgive myself. As I began to love myself, I began to desire to care for myself, and it felt really good. By taking care of myself, I was better able to care for my relationships. When we are living in a chronic state of stress, it's hard to deal with life and build relationships using ineffective stress management techniques such as drinking too much red wine and not dealing with your trauma. I was living in total survival mode. Hindsight is truly 20/20. You are making decisions from your monkey brain because of the chronic stress state you are living in. Stress causes the blood flow in your brain to be shunted away from the frontal lobe to your primitive brain, where survival is the focus—not long-term survival. It's hard to describe, but those of you who have experienced this will understand what I'm saying.

I know we see a lot of memes and quotes where it sounds like healing is all rainbows and butterflies, but this couldn't be farther from the truth. True healing is raw and dirty at times. I really have a love-hate relationship because the deeper I go with the healing, the more I find to heal. Despite being difficult at times, it really is the most beautiful part of the healing process. The chance to find out who we really are and discover how we really feel inside. It felt like I had been asleep, just going through the motions of daily life, and when I woke up, it was a huge shock!

I discovered that I'm not such a horrible person after all. I have made my share of mistakes, for sure, but inside, I am a good person. I found my inner warrior, Sephordite, through Tony Robbins and the KK Unleash Your Power training. When I begin to fear or doubt, I remind myself of my inner warrior, and it helps to conquer those old self-limiting beliefs.

As we go along the healing journey, we learn that we are unable to heal deeper layers of ourselves (I think of an onion) until we've peeled away the outer layers. This is not always easy, and sometimes we don't like what we find. It's okay because it's never too late for self-improvement. First, we must begin to love who we are, trust our inner voice, and accept where we are right now. From there, I was able to begin my journey.

I learned that many of the relationships I had witnessed growing up were not healthy relationships and had impacted me more than I realized. All of them involved addiction in at least one partner, physical or emotional abuse, or both. I began to take a look at my own life. I had been divorced twice; a single mother of six children. It was too close for comfort to my mother's life, and I had to have the courage to look at these similarities and take responsibility for my part in it.

We can only change ourselves, but imagine what a huge difference it would make to all of humanity if the whole world bought into this idea. Love is the healing balm of our Creator. It vibrates to all, but only those attuned to the frequency can hear it. Our job, then, is to help people heal so they may hear the tune.

I discovered through my healing journey that love is a verb, not a noun. I really found it through being a mother. You commit yourself to loving this being and caring for them for at least 18 years—but really for a lifetime. You love them despite sleep deprivation, teenage rebellions, addictions, and being told they hate you. I really believe that when we begin to care for and serve someone with the right motivation, we begin to love them.

Love begins with the way we talk to one another as well as holding space and showing up for one another when times get rough. Love is about commitment; we don't give up. We may have to pause and reset, but we don't give up. Love doesn't have a list of conditions that have to be met in order to be given. It's not easy to give or receive, especially if you were raised in a family where love wasn't freely expressed.

I hope you found something valuable by reading about my journey, no matter how small. I hope that if you are searching for love, you begin by loving and forgiving yourself. Remember, love is not abusive; it's not conditional, and it cannot survive in an addictive relationship unless that addiction is managed.

I'm an ordained minister and have had the privilege of marrying my sister, my daughter, and a friend's son. I would like to end by sharing a favorite scripture that I like to use when marrying couples. I like to look at this scripture as a guidepost, something to always be striving toward:

LOVE

Is Patient, Love Is Kind.
It Does Not Envy, It Does Not Boast,
It Is Not Proud. It Does Not Dishonor Others,
It Is Not Self-Seeking, It Is Not Easily Angered,
It Keeps No Record Of Wrongs.
Love Does Not Delight In Evil
But Rejoices With The Truth.
It Always Protects, Always Trusts,
Always Hopes, Always Perseveres.
LOVE NEVER FAILS

—1 Corinthians 13:4–8

About Jennifer Bassett

Jennifer is a nurse health coach and owns her own coaching business named Coach Jenny Bassett, which she launched in the Spring of 2023. She served in the United States Air Force as an officer and a nurse in the 1990s. She has six children, two adorable grandsons, a new grandbaby due in August, and an equally adorable fur baby Pug named Piper. Her family is her greatest joy.

She was diagnosed with multiple sclerosis (MS) at the age of 48, and the news came after many years of struggle and hardship as a single parent of six children. Two years after her diagnosis, she was forced to retire as a homecare nurse manager due to the progression of MS.

She felt so hopeless at one point that she thought about ending her own life. It was the love for her children and her faith that allowed her to summon the courage to face this new chapter in her life.

She no longer recognized the person she had become and was just going through the motions of life. It was when she allowed herself to forgive and love herself that she began to truly heal.

Her health and wellness journey began in 2017, and she became inspired to become a certified functional nutrition health coach when learning about the star role her fork played in managing her disease and overall health. She learned that food is the most important tool to have in her toolbox. It works better and is cheaper than many medications, with no adverse side effects.

She is an avid believer of the quote: "What you put at the end of your fork is more powerful than anything you will ever find in a prescription bottle. It works faster, better, and cheaper, and all the side effects are good ones" (Mark Hyman, MD).

For the Love of the Divine!

—

Kathleen Dutton

If HOPE was a constellation
What would it look like?
Would it be soft and mellow?
Or dark as the deepest space?
Like the Milky Way: a swirling?
Or the gentle touch of an Angel?
Heavenly or Earthly?
Would you rise from its ashes
as a God or Insect?
Would you dance for it?
Pray or
create some work of art?
Will you welcome or scorn it?
Only you can know my dear!
Sit quietly and listen.
Are you ushering it in?
Or swishing it out
with the dishwater?
Funny thing about it
is when it enters,
there's a mystery around
How it works out!

But know: you are loved.
Know, the way is clear
If you decide to take a chance
Hope is a friend;
and will guide you
out of fear.
It takes you home
so pack your bag.
This is a move: to Divine Love.

—Kathleen Dutton

Shhhh! It's "Love" but not as we know it!

I always loved the "Star Trek" television series, a favorite show of my child-hood days. How they encountered the amazing realms and different life forms on the Starship Enterprise. How Scotty the Medic would say, "It's life, Captain, but not as we know it!" … It raises the question about both our assumptions about life and what our expectations are and how they show up in the world. It's actually loaded with wisdom, and you could actually write a whole book on the idea of that.

Today, I'm going to be concise and write a chapter about the hidden realm of love: an invisible force that is part of us all and one of our orig-inal soul qualities, very powerful. It brings the heart alive gently or with exploding eruptions of joy: when a new baby is born, in their eyes, you see it, fresh and bright. It's that big love that stirs us into action for our hu-manity and is the glue that unites our life force with those around us, our brothers and sisters in the earthly realm, to find that love within—well, that's the most powerful one of all, healing wounds and a salve to the soul.

In the creation stories, the attraction of love binds us into the physical form of the things that are in plain sight in our own lives. I can go to a place, see a person, or appreciate a piece of art, and it's extraordinary to think of each person who is witnessing what's right in front of them in a completely different way. We are all engaging with reality according to our own knowledge, experience, and inner guidance system that charges that perception through our very unique soul qualities. That being said, I'm going to speak a little about my own quest for "The Love of the Divine" peeping through the corridors of myth, the magic, and the mystery of the hidden realms. How it set me free from my own illusion. Then to see the world through the eyes of love. There is something about the healing voice as a tool to that connection, as a way to tune into those hidden realms, and as a gateway of transformation. Truly, as that happened, the whole world seemed to alchemize and become both an exciting and soothing quest for the deeper aspects of myself.

Below is a dream that woke me at 3 a.m. At the same time, the eclipse doorway of the Schumann resonance was really high over the last few days; I'd describe it as the heartbeat of our amazing planet that could connect with all life here. Usually, it has a steady rhythm, but today, its rhythm did something that it has never done before. The Earth's frequency data created a whole new pattern and colors. We've had lots more electromagnetic vibrations surround and affect us as humans as the planets line up, and the elements of life are stirred. Mother Earth's natural heartbeat rhythm is the frequency, also known as the "Schumann Resonance"; that 7.83 Hz frequency is an alpha/theta brainwave frequency in the human brain. Alpha/Theta brainwave frequency is a relaxed, dreamy, sleepy state that is also when cell regeneration and healing happens.

It is no surprise that people nowadays, especially in bigger cities, are unbalanced, irritated, reactive, and angry, and diseases are rising in astronomical numbers. We live in a time of technology, with superficial wavelengths that disrupt the natural Earth's frequency. Wi-Fi, cell phones, and an array of electronics are part of our everyday lives. Is it also why our bio-electromagnetic waves are out of balance? We are out of balance with Earth's electromagnetic frequency. For example, the frequency of radiofrequency electromagnetic radiation (what powers cell phones, TVs, radio, etc.) ranges from 30,000 Hz to 300 billion Hz. That is a significant amount, more than 7.83 Hz that the earth radiates. No wonder we are all out of balance and crave healing. I'm writing more about these frequencies for my next book. I've also been creating a study of solar flares which are active at this time and how they affect consciousness through art and a few words. This is a love letter from the Divine. Speak love.

Dear SOUL,

It's time to embrace your words. See them as an activation frequency. Do you know how?

The answer is to only speak the frequency of words that you wish to create and unite all aspects of your divine self. Soul consciousness can be in your mind by dropping into your heart, and then guidance and signs appear. Have appreciation that you are on the right path. Know, when you speak what is unwanted, you feed it, except that it is a navigation system: Do hold space in you for what you want and place loving detachment in the space. Be gentle with yourself and friends for that; it's going to be interesting. You will learn a lot. Our souls have a frequency of the divine blueprint; tune in. Tap into fun on the way.

The human body carries the frequency of how it's charged. Therefore, what your previous thoughts have created; they show up now as a manifestation. The power to decide to do things differently; the power to allow that to be. However, speak new words to bless your life, to create the resonance of what's already flowing to you. In this world you live, you are really creating your reality. Your words have weight.

What words would you place here ...? On the dotted line. Those words actually become the very frequency you will attract.

Each person is a soul, and you are a soul with your own path. Creator, what are you creating? Are you creating love? If you are creating love for yourself, you are also creating more love in the Universe. Magical!

If you say, "I want to be healthy," then you create more of that WANT to be healthy. That is not an accurate description; discern. Use "I am healthy"; "I am peace"; your body will hear and respond in kind.

An illness presents an opportunity to see, feel, and accept the vibration of what is not wanted so that the higher self can heal the physical vessel. What is pain? It's a prompt to change. Listen to the message; choose wellness. With others, speak of the times they are well and be enthusiastic about that. Things work out in divine order for your soul.

Say, "Thank you, this is working out for me." Know that is true. Say less until you really get this … do less until you feel joy and inspiration carry you on a wave.

Things are always working out for you … Thoughts become things …

Balance: choose stillness, choose love, choose positive thoughts. Retrain monkey mind kindly!

You are Love.

The Catalyst of Love

When we go back in time to look at the spirit of how myth and creation dance together, it is love. The one thing that seems to unite all stories is the concept of "Divine Love"; this is love between humanity and the source of life. The one that became two, that became the expansion of all life. The idea of the uncarved block, the blank page, the thing that unites us, is the potential of energy. To me, that describes the catalyst that is soul sovereign divinity, the highest love with great power of the potential for creating.

The first mission of exploration was of my own roots in London and

Essex during a challenging time for me. In *Mission Hope, Volume I*, I took the idea of the "Australian Soul Songlines" with me … the song of my own life story, honoring the past and ancestors of those lands. In the same way, the ancients took of the depth of what is, a mound, a river, the sea, the history behind our urban sprawl of the city. It's a deep dive that takes us through to the very heart of these realms … beyond the concrete and asphalt, remembering the layers of time, of what the land and indigenous ancient cultures witnessed and how it was part of the creation story. That is part of what I'm interested in exploring here. It's the narratives, the birth of life that sparks up from and builds the sacred within the spirit of the land. In that is the connection to us all as beings on this earth.

In the last Mission Hope book, *Volume II*, I explored the idea of "The Battle of Woe and Hope" in Avalon. There is the portal of presence that is somehow part of the multidimensional realm. Some people say it is located in another world; others say that it is an ideal land, a place of the imagination. Some say it was a real place, which cannot now be found. In a sense, it's an inner place … part of the esoteric plane of existence … in the same way that Glastonbury is a very down-to-earth town with a Boots the Chemist, a butcher, a baker, a candlestick maker, but it is also Avalon. Avalon the myth meets the mystical and magical home of the Tor, Chalice Well, and the Abbey, and my favorite place to retreat is at St Margaret's Chapel.

Avalon is a mythical island featured in the Arthurian Legend. It first appeared in Geoffrey of Monmouth's 1136 Historia Regum Britanniae as a place of magic where King Arthur's sword Excalibur was made and later where Arthur was taken to recover from being gravely wounded at the Battle of Camlann.

Singing At The Well

As I turn my attention inward
The wind blows on my skin
Birds sing
I voice my heart-song

A rainbow expands
I am attuned
To the simplicity

of the inner being.
Shafts of light dance
I am love
In this moment
All is well.

—*Kathleen Dutton*

In this chapter, we delve into the concepts of love and an inner quest to stoke the fire of it! It's the discovery and joy of life, along with the flame of energy of nurturing it within, instead of seeking it externally. I've been using it for many years. I use it in combination with prayer, Qi Gong, and particular mantras that I learned when I lived in Hong Kong, but it was originally from Tibet. I use it while meditating as well as creating my own free-flow songs and drawings to seal the bond. There was healing from a critical illness and a disease of patterns and pain. There were rainbows all around me as I sat in that stillness, a celebration within. A deep gratitude for this new chapter I get to live and write about with you now.

It was just after I got the all-clear from my scan. I'm not going to go into that part now, as I do believe that I give energy and words to what is wanted … (not to what is unwanted: the inner guidance is only to give attention to what is wanted). To feed the energies of what is healthy and beautiful, fade what is out of alignment. As a friend, I will say that it was while in the depths of my own peace and silence that a transformation occurred. So, I began my physical journey to go home on trains, everything a feeling of lightness in my step. There was a sense of a new start during my last few moments of being in Avalon at Glastonbury Station. On my return trip, I was there to say thank you to Avalon for being a sanctuary for my connection to divine source energy, peace, health, and joy; to say thank you for my life in the place where I'd sought that calm connection to nature, my inner being, a return to love, and offering my days as a more humble, joyous, and dedicated human being.

As I sat at the station, I received a call inviting me to go to the home of Buddhism. It was a piece of synchro-destiny and a bolt from the blue; some strings of the energy field of what has been part of my practice for decades. Suddenly, I'm just in awe of the wonder at the power of this moment. I booked my tickets and had a feeling of the "majesty of the mystery." So, what next?

Shhh ... Shekinah on the quest for Shambhala?

In the quest for Shambhala, I knew the word I had the notion of what in English is an expression that we use to describe a place, as a kind of paradise of sorts. I had thought it was a real place. I knew the word as a child. It was exotic and magical in my mind. Full of Eastern promise. The question is, is Shambhala a real place? Nowadays, no one knows where Shambala is...

Although it is said to exist, people cannot see it or communicate with it in an ordinary way.

There was a sense of something to be learned, a deeper understanding of the power of our intentions and love uniting on a golden pathway that takes the soul home to its real homeland of the higher self and that powerful source of purification and the divine spirit of all that is.

It's for us; it's for me, and I've got my whole new vision coming into sight. It's only now that I realize the threads of that divine feminine power are rising, and one of the most potent mantras is The Green Tara mantra ... a female personification of the Buddha. Once again, this brings us into that divine feminine nurturing energy to charge it with the recognition of the rebalancing of this energy within.

I have been doing paintings and drawings around the idea of the principal idea of the Shekinah as the indwelling presence and feminine potency of that goddess. It's curious that the narratives of the Virgin Mary,

Mary Magdalene, and the Black Madonna arose and spread throughout Europe. It was here the troubadours and poets and others sang their songs of devotion to the feminine principle and wrote their fables of the Holy Grail. It seems that the rise of our own feminine energies is healing. The discovery of "The Gospel of Mary" and its teachings increase awareness around this aspect of ourselves. No matter whether we are a man or a woman, we have experienced the women in our lives, and it is through our experience of how culture nurtures the feminine aspect for more love in our world at this time that has created a shadow.

As we reframe how Mary Magdalene is considered, its in leaving behind the old story, taking a cue from the Catholic, Orthodox, Anglican, and Lutheran churches who already consider her to be a Saint, with a feast day of July 22, which, funny enough, is a significant day for me, as it's my own mother's birthday; so, I've been celebrating this day my whole life. The Eastern Orthodox churches also commemorate her on the Sunday of the Myrrh bearers, the Orthodox equivalent of the Western Three Marys.

In apocryphal texts, Mary is portrayed as a visionary and leader of the early movement whom Jesus loved more than He loved the other disciples. Several Gnostic gospels, such as the Gospel of Mary, written in the early 2nd century, see Mary as the special disciple of Jesus who has a deeper understanding of His teachings and is asked to impart this to the other disciples. That is why she was later also called "Apostle of the Apostles." Later still in her life, Mary Magdalene is said to have lived in the South of France and died there. One of my life missions is to go there. It's interesting to note that relics of hers are said to have been taken to Vezelay, where they were kept in the Crypt of the Basilica.

In the assembled texts within the Bible, it's hard to find positive examples of the female who is having a healthy relationship with God and their partners; the example of a loving partner or wife is missing; the prostitute or the mother archetype is present. In some ways, I have a sense that adding the Gospel of Mary would add balance. In other cultures, we find that the feminine was honored, first and foremost, as being the one who gives actual physical birth to life and also as the primary nurturing of Mother Earth—that connection to her. It's also in the indigenous culture of faith that brings Mother Earth and Father Sky together as part of a sacred dance with life and the source love energy, God.

As I come into more balance within, we respect all life and each voice as part of the whole. That is to do with direct connection as opposed to one of subservience.

> *Shechinah (Hebrew: na'av Shina) is the English transliteration of a Hebrew word meaning „dwelling" or „settling" and denotes the presence of God, as it were, in a place. This concept is found in Judaism. The Hebrew Bible mentions several places where the presence of God was felt and experienced as a Shekhinah, including the burning bush and the cloud that rested on Mount Sinai. The Shekhinah was often pictured as a cloud or as a pillar of fire.*
> —*Extract from Wikipedia*

Mary Magdalene or Mary of Magdala (and sometimes The Magdalene) was one of Jesus' most celebrated disciples and the most important female disciple in the movement of Jesus. Jesus cleansed her of seven demons, sometimes interpreted as referring to complex illnesses. She became Jesus' close friend and was most prominent during His last days.

When Jesus was crucified by the Romans, Mary Magdalene was there, supporting Him. She stayed with Him at the cross after the male disciples. She was at His burial. In all four New Testament gospels, Mary Magdalene is the first to arrive at Jesus' tomb, where she encounters an angel who instructs her to go tell the disciples that Jesus has risen. She was very connected to her own spiritual world and had her own gospel.

In the Quest for Shambhala

Come - A - Come - A - Come- A- Shambhala !!!
There was a healing
All the mother energy
all that is feminine too.

The way that we
humanity: each soul
dances with that aspect.
Hitting the collective
as a wave.
The way we nurture.
How we show up:
To self-soothe.
Supreme being
as an eternal flame.
Support is given
to the mother-lines
through the divine father-lines
we are all connected to
these higher timelines
 of parenthood
shine like ribbons of Hope
throughout all time in space
this is done.

The wound of oppression
of suppressing
of rage and worry
where the Mothers within
and in that role
did not act from Love.
The highest good
swirling in the milk
into the Milky Way.
Balance that; the over
and under feeding
The slap of frustration seen.
The cry for help as the children
and the inner children

call this healing into our bloodlines.
Into the Human spirit
So the wise woman rises
of female sovereignty.
The soft light and gentle
voice of Mother Mary
Says "Let it be."
Green Tara clapped
her hands and put her
left foot forward.
Ready to spring into action.

—Kathleen Dutton

Honestly, there is a sense that many things will work if you feel and believe it. To explore is to adore. We all have our own way to get there. I feel the pull toward overtone chanting that is practiced in both as part of the Tibetan Buddhist mantra and also Gregorian chant in terms of its resonances to the ear and soul. Certainly, it was the central tradition of Western plainchant, a form of monophonic, unaccompanied sacred song in Latin (and occasionally Greek) of the Roman Catholic Church. Gregorian chants developed mainly in western and central Europe during the 9th and 10th centuries. I'm sure that there are many ways to sing to the world. It's through that soothing song and the divine connection either alone or—but more especially—those we create together.

On that note, I wish you well and that you enjoy your own healing and my show and tell of a snapshot of my own on the path to divine love and a sacred partnership that starts within, that follows your own unique journey "for the love of the Divine."

In the Tibetan Buddhist tradition: "Shambhala (Sanskrit: Śambhala, also spelled Shambala or Shamballa, Tibetan). Sanskrit name is taken from the name of a city mentioned in the Hindu Puranas, probably in reference to Sambhal in Uttar Pradesh. The mythological relevance of the place originates with a prophecy in Vishnu Purana according to which Shambhala will be the birthplace of Kalki, the next incarnation of Vishnu, who will usher in a new age (Satya Yuga) and the prophesied ruling Kingdom of Maitreya, the future Buddha" (Extract from Wikipedia).

A gateway of higher vibration is open; call it what feels accurate. Shambhala, Paradise, The Golden Age; it's part of the planet, of divine order; it's part of you. Love is at the core. "Love is the answer," and I embrace it as an energetic field. The universe reinforces the wonder of that enchantment, the message of the soul's song, that love is the key to all of life's problems. It serves as a reminder that we may think we have all the answers, but ultimately, it is love that will guide us. That is the final mystery.

All love,
Kathleen Dutton

About Kathleen Dutton

Kathleen, a creative soul, infuses joy into life through her art, events, and courses, emphasizing fun and inner exploration. Her current focus involves co-creating in diverse settings, blending creativity, healing, and the arts at local and international levels. Kathleen, featured on BBC Radio and Sky TV, is a regular speaker at international conferences, conducting workshops that integrate creativity, well-being, storytelling, imagination, and the healing arts.

Her journey spans 19 years at Skylark Galleries, Southbank, London, where she founded Earth Altera, fostering creativity through drawing and collage. A founder member of Earth Altera, Kathleen initiated an international project for creating sacred spaces in nature. Noteworthy projects include collaborative efforts on cross-cultural branding designs and upcoming book releases.

Kathleen's expertise extends to creative project partnerships, graphic design, illustration storyboards, animations, and artist-in-residence roles with UAL, Oxo Tower, RSL Collective, Brent Arts, and Libraries. Notably, she contributed to a play bus project addressing isolation, particularly among mother and baby groups and special needs communities. Another impactful endeavor involved art creation with drawing, movement, and sound healing through music at "spirited bodies."

Her accolades include fellowships from the Society of Designers and The Kings Fund of Great Britain. Kathleen is adept at setting up and advising social enterprises, recognized for pioneering leadership at the grassroots level, including projects with the Royal Festival Hall and various art and community centers. She spearheaded initiatives for the homeless and the elderly, collaborating with the Big Issue as an artist in residence.

Beyond London, Kathleen served as the Beach Hut Artist in Essex for Tendring Council. Her rich life experience encompasses a passion for ancient cultures, international travels, and residences expressed through art, illustration, and writing in sketchbooks. As an author, Kathleen is on her third book in the Mission Hope series, embodying roles as a catalyst, healing circle facilitator, mother, and teacher.

Kathleen's educational background includes a BA in graphic design from Middlesex University and an MA in visual communications from the University of Central England. She lectured at the University of Westminster, London, and Hong Kong Polytechnic University, contributing seven years as a graphic design lecturer in Hong Kong and nine years at Conran Design Group.

Constantly curious about healing energy, Kathleen holds qualifications as a Theta healer, sound healer, and Reiki healer and delves into the study of the Schumann Resonance and Solar Flares. Her multifaceted journey encapsulates a commitment to creativity, community, and holistic well-being.

My Way Toward Love

Alexia Avila

Dear Reader, you may not recognize me. To you, I am just a stranger who is expressing parts of herself she never thought had a space to thrive. You see, for me, this life has been anything but linear, smooth, and as expected. The best word I can use to express my growth throughout most of my time here is turbulent, exhausting, yet rewarding. Now, I am not here to facilitate a vibe of negativity or selfishness. I am here to tell a story, one I have been waiting to tell my whole life. One that resonates with me so deeply that it is transformative and must come to the surface to unfold … a story so deep in the depths of my soul that I have waited 25 years of my life to find a place for it. And let me preface this, I have always had a hunger, a need, and a "mission" (if you will) to help those who have gone through a similar life path as me. I know I am not alone. And with that, I want you to know you, too, are not alone and never will be.

I am not where I want to be quite yet in my life to tell this story. If I am honest, I want to inspire others, and sometimes, it takes overcoming my challenges to be able to do so. I have some extra unhealthy weight on me, haven't pursued my passions to the degree I'd hoped as a youngster, and could have told you yesterday I was not happy at all with who I am. However, I will not let those things define or stop me because, really, all we have is now, and now is infinitely subjective. I once heard a quote that said, "Treat every day like a Monday; treat every month like a January."

Every day you are living is a new chance to choose love, to choose happiness, to choose peace, and to just be present. Presence is where peace lies, where love lies. Love conquers all. We are more powerful than we know.

Today is January 1st, 2024, and I have decided to switch some things up in my life. Yesterday was rough, last year was rough, and life has been tough, but going forward, I am choosing to consciously decide that today and this year will simply not be that same way. All of my life, I have used my circumstances to define me, and that simply is no longer resonating. I have finally made a decision to be done with constant suffering and all the negativity that I have previously allowed to take over my current existence. I am embarking on a new journey without expectations and regardless of the outcome. I am going to start to alter my mindset and positively shift my focus toward actually living and loving my life.

Life isn't simple or easy, but it doesn't have to be hard. And yes, I am aware I may face more hardship going forward. But today, I am choosing to consciously be aware and see past my current situation to manifest a better reality because, in my case, I have always let history, conditions, or even yesterday define my identity and life. This way of thinking, or over-thinking, has gone on far too long in my case. Today, at this moment, I am choosing peace and love; I am choosing to embark upon my mission, and that begins with me. Let me tell you a little more about what I've been through that has led me to this point.

I grew up in a quaint, small town in New Jersey known as Demarest. I had what seemed to be, at the time, insurmountable depression and a compulsion to over-consuming my food. These behaviors did not come about for no reason, though. In what seemed to be just a matter of months, it became the only way I knew how to cope. I was 17; my father had just passed away, and my family and I lost our house, the place I grew up and spent just about all my childhood and beyond. This was my "home."

I already had some residual trauma I faced as a kid, but by this point, my life seemed as though it had completely spun out of control. By my early 20s, I had lost all hope of anything ever getting better, and that lasted for quite some time. For years, I used bingeing as a method to cope because it brought me comfort. I also used Obsessive Compulsive Disease, known as OCD, as a method of trying to stop the constant changes in my life. This had proven itself to be impossible.

These compulsions made me feel as though I had some sense of control in a very turbulent and overwhelming reality. I strongly believed that if I had washed my hands enough or retraced my steps while taking a walk to get from point A to point B, I could have prevented anything else horrible from happening, like death, per se, because, after all, my dad had passed. How could I be sure my mom or brother wouldn't be next? My intrusive thoughts began to take me over the edge to the point where I completely lost my sense of identity. I felt as though I was torturing myself to prevent anything else bad from happening. I even had to take some time in a psychiatric hospital to attempt to begin a recovery, which helped for a while, until I decided it was time to return.

Through all of the craziness, I would turn to music as a channel to express my discomfort, sadness, grief, and slew of emotions I had been feeling during this period. After all, my happiest moments in childhood involved singing or dancing. I love to sing. It has always been my haven through the dark; my channel music is the reason I chose to keep going or even be alive. Singing turned into songwriting, and songwriting turned into constant practicing until I came up with a full composition titled "My Way." This song is all about the suffering I was going through, as well as the lack of friends I had at the time and a good support system. It was all about reaching the other side through dark times, overcoming hardship, and choosing to own my way of healing. So, I kept my head held high through all of this. I confided in my family and my art and coped through my pain, knowing I had something better unfolding.

I have recently realized that even through all these harsh circumstances and trauma, I am here and OK right now, and I have accomplished so much, despite what that negative voice in my head always tries to tell me. I conclude, there must be a reason I am still alive. Today is January

12, 2024; I'm 25 years old (soon to be 26), capable and healthy enough, maybe not in the healthiest physique of my life quite yet, but I have health; I have legs, and I can walk. I have a working brain, and I am not physically ill in any way right now, although I am recovering from COVID-19 I contracted from another family member, who was more ill than I am right now, but I am in good health and slowly but surely recovering.

I am faithful not only in the possibilities of the future but also in the here and now. I am whole, able, and willing to create a better life for myself and believe I can have a positive impact on the world by following my dreams and spreading my light through my mission of writing songs and writing my story in this book to help other people who are in the same shoes as I have been. This is where I start. I have a full heart, and I am gifted, and I am willing to finally decide to use it not only for my greatest potential and highest good but for the good of the world by extending my love and light outward. I am recognizing my worth, living my full potential, and starting afresh with a new mindset because I have all the tools I need. Every day is a new opportunity to become a better version of myself. I am becoming more conscious, kind, and loving to myself, which is reflected in those around me as well. This is what got me through my songwriting journey, and my pain, and this is how I am starting to show up for the world. This is the power of love.

Love is not even just a mere act or a romantic feeling. Love can be found everywhere—in the trees, in the sun, all around us, and even in a breath of fresh air or a cup of coffee. There is an infinite supply of love in this world, enough for everyone. You do not need a romantic partner or a date to roll around to access love. Love is within us; love is everywhere. It is our natural state. And yes, the world may not be as simple as we had hoped for as children or feel as playful. But it is up to us to keep our inner child close to our hearts because our inner child is us in our purest form—our higher self, you may call it. It is us before we learn the ways of the world.

This earth plane is meant for expressing ourselves, dancing, playing, and loving. Reality is our canvas. Unfortunately, every day, negative occurrences happen in this world, a lot of which obviously may be out of our control. But what we can do is continue to stay positive despite it all. The universal hardship that is in the world is uncanny right now. There is constant death, wars, loss, major world changes, distance from loved ones, isolation, loneliness, depression … but they are nothing new. These are some of the many things we are experiencing on this earth every day throughout the lives we live. We all feel it as a part of the collective, for we are all one and affected on some level by the lives around us, whether we are aware or not.

This is the time that we must not let the darkness win. We must stand taller and hold love even closer, standing strong in the power of love through the face of adversity. Martin Luther King once said, "Hate cannot drive out hate; only love can do that. Darkness can not drive out dark; only light can do that." When we continue to go forth, despite pain and hopelessness, only then will we pave the way for more light to come in. We can overcome the darkness and suffering only when the dark is brought to the light. As humans, we are capable of creating anything we direct our sights on. So, we must act in faith and have trust in something greater, and the light will always supersede the dark. In physics, light overpowers the darkness. If you plug in a lamp, the light comes on. Dark becomes light; pain can be lifted, and sorrow can be shifted. It is only when we see dark, we know the sun will still rise.

Veering back to my journey, I have finally made a vow to myself to take a new path of understanding and end the miserable compulsions of a few years back. Now, I am also putting an end to any residual impulsive behaviors such as overeating and overspending that have bled into my more recent adulthood. They are no longer resonating with me. Through love, I have found there is so much more good out there in this life. Today, I am grateful that every day alive is a new chance for gratitude, happiness, and love to just be without any expectation or sense of past or future; just here and now where life is infinitely bountiful and imperfectly beautiful because presence is where peace lies. And when we create space for that, we create space for love and project it out into our surroundings. So today, I am choosing to start believing in the possibility of every day and just take everything one moment at a time. Love starts within.

I've always wanted to make this world a better place than it was before I left it. Painting pictures through words and instilling hope in others makes life so much more fulfilling for me. This is the day I have chosen to be a living, breathing example of picking up the pieces and choosing to live my life fully. I am choosing love over and over through my words, actions, and feelings, knowing it all starts with me. Ah, I am finding love through the power of music and extending that out into the world for people to find hope through the dark times.

I promise you, no matter how much pain you are facing, consistent struggle, or heartbreak, it can and WILL ALWAYS get better so long as you believe that. I want you to know you are never alone in your struggles, and you are so much more than the experiences you have gone through or the circumstances you are currently facing. You are a living, breathing soul full of light and love. Anything is possible in the light of love. "God has never and will never forsake you; I have chosen you and not rejected you; So do not fear, for I am with you." Every time you feel like giving up, I hope you will refer to this chapter. And remember, the power of love is always within.

Sincerely,
Alexia Avila

> *And I can see clearly now.*
> *There's so much to be seen*
> *that's never been seen before*
> *... I'm walking in sun,*
> *And I'm pushing through rain.*
> *I'm wishing for love,*
> *But until that day,*

I ain't going to give up.
I'm walking my way right now,
And I won't let up
'Cause I'm living …
My way.
—Alexia Avila (extracted from the original song "My Way"; MP3
available everywhere now)

About Alexia Avila

Alexia Avila, a New York-born singer, songwriter, mental health advocate, and first-time author, has been creating her whole life. She is best known for her works in music and entertainment but is no stranger to writing. She has attended Baldwin Wallace University, where she was a part of the Voices of Praise Gospel Choir (Featured on Fox 5 TV), as well as the prestigious Berklee College of Music 5-week program. Alexia, 25, recently moved to Brea, California, where she now resides to focus on her personal journey and career. She has served her community and volunteered to work with individuals on the spectrum. Alexia has a strong affinity for mental health, and her mission is to inspire those who have been through dark times to feel heard, seen, and less alone in the world. Through her musical work, as well as written work, she aims to come from a very genuine place in her heart to inspire and give a voice to individuals who feel misunderstood. Alexia Avila is very excited to be an author taking part in the very powerful, prophetic, and cathartic experience: *Mission Hope, The Power of Love.*

Blessed With Love

———

Dobby Webb

Childhood Love

My whole life has been blessed by love in one form or another, and I am so very grateful! My parents were college sweethearts who married in 1956 and were married for 55 years before we lost my mother to lung cancer. My mom was actually engaged to someone from her hometown, and her then-current fiancé heard that my father, who was a friend of his from college, would be going to her hometown during the summer, and he suggested my father look up his fiancée and say hello while he was in town … and my father got the girl! While my parents had ups and downs during their 55 years together, they loved each other and their children. They had their hands full with four children born in four years.

Growing up, my parents were involved in all of our activities. They attended PTA meetings and were Brownie leaders, Cub Scout leaders, and Boy Scout leaders. While we did not have a lot of money, we had a lot of love and a lot of fun! We camped out quite often, and I believe that we camped at every Arkansas State Park Campground that was around back then. My father worked in the family business (a local funeral home) until the year that I graduated from high school; then he did a couple of other jobs before settling in working for the Arkansas State Department of Parks and Tourism. My mom was a stay-at-home mom until I was in junior high school; then she worked at a plant shop for a couple of years, and then for decades at a family-owned and run jewelry store.

Growing up, we lived in the BEST neighborhood that had six man-made lakes, a swimming pool, tennis courts, baseball/softball fields, and playgrounds. One of the lakes is specifically for boating and water skiing. Another was specifically for swimming. They must have trucked in loads of sand to create a graduated slope so that the sandy area was great for small children to build sandcastles and to be able to sit in just a few inches of water and splash to their heart's content. We spent many happy days at the lake and the pool. As each of us hit about age six, we each began taking Red Cross swim lessons—Beginners and Advanced Beginners were taught at the lake; then Intermediate and Swimmers were taught at the pool. Growing up in our neighborhood during these years was such an awesome experience; I loved every minute of it!

Christian Love

As we were growing up, our maternal grandparents lived in Wichita Falls, Texas, so we did not see them very often. However, we spent a lot of time with our paternal grandparents, whom we called Mom and Doe, and our great-aunt. We went to church with our grandparents or great-aunt, then went to our great-aunt's house for lunch, and then to our grandparent's house for dinner and to watch Wonderful World of Disney on their color TV set (we had a black and white TV set back then). Our grandmother passed away when I was six, and that ended the Sunday tradition of lunch at our great-aunt's and dinner at our grandparent's houses …yet a new tradition was born. Our great-aunt began picking up my brothers and me on Sunday mornings, taking us to Sunday school and church, out to lunch, and then back to her house to play for the afternoon. As children, we absolutely LOVED our time with our great-aunt! Besides the fun we had, it provided my foundation of faith in God. The lessons I learned growing up going to Sunday school, church, vacation Bible school in the summers, and singing in the church choir as I got older have held me on a good path for the rest of my life. I know that God created me, Jesus gave His life on the cross to save my life and wash me clean of my sins, and that the Holy Spirit lives in me. I also know that there have been a few times in my life that the "Footprints in the Sand" poem has played out in my life when Jesus carried me in His arms and allowed me the time to rest and heal. I firmly believe that I am still alive, as God still has plans for me here on Earth.

Brotherly Love

It's funny how my brothers and I followed the same path in many ways in our growing-up years. The boys played baseball and were in Boy Scouts. I played softball and was in Girl Scouts. We, all four, took additional Red Cross advanced lessons so that we could volunteer and teach all six levels of Red Cross swim lessons at our neighborhood pool and lake. We all were lifeguards at both the lake and the pool. We all went to the University of Arkansas at Little Rock. I am still close with all of my brothers and treasure my relationships with them!

Romantic Love

When I was a freshman in college, I was surprised that the fraternity men hosted something called "The Toilet Bowl," which was a powder puff football game where the sororities played flag football, and the frat pledges dressed up as cheerleaders. Some of the frat members were assigned to each sorority as football coaches. James Webb was one of our coaches, which was how I met my future husband. We were each dating someone else when we met, but we became good friends. A few months later, we went shopping to get Valentine's Day gifts ... him shopping for his then-girlfriend, and me for my then-boyfriend. The next month, I broke up with my boyfriend, then James ended up solo, and we have been together ever since. We got married on March 3, 1979; so, by the time this book is in print, we will have just celebrated our 45th wedding anniversary!

When James and I got married, I thought we would always live in the Little Rock area, but over the years, we have moved multiple times with his work. We have lived in 15 cities so far.

Love for Our Babies

Our plan was to wait five years to start a family, but life did not go according to our plan. Our first daughter was born four days before our first wedding anniversary. James got a promotion about the same time that our oldest daughter was born; therefore, we moved to Texas, and he began traveling the states of Arkansas, Louisiana, Texas, Oklahoma, and New Mexico. This meant that I was home alone with a new baby the majority of the time. Quite a lot to take on at the young age of 20.

Our oldest daughter was only six months old when we found out that we were expecting again. Our second daughter was born when our oldest daughter was 15 months old; so, having two in diapers was a challenge—especially with James traveling every week. My sweet husband found a way to let me sleep all night when he was in town since I was the one who got up with the girls during the night Monday through Friday. I breastfed each of our babies; so, when he heard one crying, he would go change her diaper, bring her into our room, allow her to nurse for approximately 10 minutes, burp her, roll me to the other side, let her nurse for another 10 minutes, burp her again, and put her back in her crib. I was so exhausted on those days that I slept right through the whole process.

Our only son came along when the girls were two and three years old. James was still traveling and helped with the overnight feedings again. I thought I was tired with one, then two; now, with two toddlers and a newborn, I seemed to be exhausted most of the time, but they say that each new phase is just a different challenge. As our oldest started kindergarten, life eased up a little bit. The next year, our youngest daughter started kindergarten, and I actually got to have some one-on-one time with our son. I was a little sad when he started kindergarten, but life keeps moving on. Elementary school, then junior high; then it seemed like it was just a blink of an eye, and our oldest daughter was graduating from high school. Our younger daughter graduated the following year, and our son two years later.

Love through "In Sickness and In Health"

While we lived in the Kansas City area, James' cardiologist found three blockages in his heart, and he had to have bypass surgery. This was the first big health challenge that we had faced, and it was pretty scary! Luckily, James had a wonderful surgeon, and the procedure went just as planned. I was able to stay with him overnight in the hospital for his three-day stay and help him with everything he needed there and for the next three weeks at home. James participated in cardiac rehab, which helped his recovery time immensely. That was in June, and in November of the same year, I was diagnosed with breast cancer. I had a surgical biopsy that confirmed cancer, a lumpectomy that did not get a clear margin—meaning there was still more cancer in there—so I had to have a second lumpectomy where they did get a clear margin. This was followed by six and a half weeks of radiation, which ended up being the most painful part of the whole ordeal, as my skin burned and peeled repeatedly. This was definitely our most challenging year to date!

Fifteen years after surviving breast cancer, a new breast cancer was discovered. While my first experience was relatively mild in retrospect, this time was much more serious—Stage 3 Invasive Ductal Carcinoma. I had six rounds of chemotherapy, a lumpectomy to make sure the central area showed no more cancer, radiation, and a mastectomy with reconstruction. During the timeframe of radiation, I also ended up with an autoimmune disease called Chronic Inflammatory Demyelinating Polyneuropathy that caused my body to attack and destroy all the protective coverings of every nerve in my body. It began with the "pins and needles" feeling that you get when you have your legs crossed too long, then progressed into dropping things, stumbling, falling, and finally being in a wheelchair. Within a few weeks, I went from feeling normal to being paralyzed from the neck down. James was such a trooper through the whole thing—from breast cancer to being paralyzed! He took such good care of me, getting up early to get me bathed and dressed, learning how to wash and dry my hair and put it up in a ponytail, and feeding me. He even tried putting makeup on for me so that I would look nice for a friend's birthday party ... but he decided he should wash off the makeup before going out in public. That›s what I call love!

During that very difficult time, I had to have care 24 hours a day. Rather than being placed in a nursing home, I had an awesome group of family and friends who came and took care of me during the day while James had to be at work. I am forever grateful that they loved me and were willing to take care of me so that I did not have to go to a nursing home! Through the grace of God, I was blessed to have two wonderful neurologists taking care of me during the struggles I faced with Chronic Inflammatory Demyelinating Polyneuropathy. The first neurologist was so diligent in his research to determine what the actual diagnosis was, and then he referred me to a muscular neurologist, who thankfully had treated someone with the same autoimmune disease the year before. He prescribed a wonder drug called IVIG to be administered via IV every three weeks for a full year, then every four weeks for the second year, and then every five weeks for the third year. With these treatments and months of both physical therapy and occupational therapy, I am now considered to be in remission from the CIDP.

Love for Our Grandchildren

Our oldest daughter got married shortly after James had his bypass, and my breast cancer, and the following year, we were blessed with our first grandson. Grandchildren are full of love and so much fun. Our daughters got together and chose our grandparent names—Papa and Grammy. Our oldest daughter and her husband welcomed baby boy number two just over two years later. Having two grandsons was twice the fun. Mom and Dad were incredibly surprised a couple of years later to find out that they were expecting again …with twins! Big brothers were five and three when their identical baby brothers were born. I got to double my grand-children›s love in one fell swoop. My vacation time that year could not have come at a better time, as I was able to stay at the hospital and help her with the twins.

Our younger daughter met and married an active-duty Navy SEAL. She moved to Virginia Beach, Virginia, where her husband was stationed. They welcomed a sweet little boy the following year. Our son-in-law was injured overseas and was medically retired from the Navy. They moved to the DFW area for our son-in-law to get his master's degree, and we were thrilled to have them close by. They welcomed their second son just before Big Brother turned four. A couple of years later, our oldest daughter and her hubby and their boys also moved to the DFW area. Having two of our children and all six of our grandsons within 15 minutes of our house made this Grammy and Papa quite happy! Our son is still in Kansas City but comes down for Christmas when work allows.

We have been so blessed to be able to spend quite a bit of time with our grandsons—babysitting, having the boys for sleepovers at our house, going to ball games, school performances, choir concerts, band concerts, etc. Christmas is my favorite holiday, and we have Christmas at our house with all of our children and all six of our grandsons every year. Our house is always decorated from top to bottom, and we try to carry on some old traditions and add some new ones as well—making sugar cookies and decorating them, decorating a gingerbread house, and making new Christmas ornaments for the tree.

Time has been marching on, and our sweet grandsons are growing up so fast. James Cole just turned 20, and we are so proud of the path he has chosen—to be a Marine. He came out of boot camp as a squad leader and an expert marksman. He was just recently promoted to Lance Corporal. Ethan is 17 and looking forward to graduating from high school soon. Caleb and Kyle are 14 and will be transitioning to high school next year. We hope that they will continue to excel in band! Gunner is 10 and enjoys riding his dirt bike and playing basketball. Lincoln is six and enjoys riding his go-cart and playing baseball. Our family is so special to us! We love them all. Family is so important; however, remember to always put God first, family second, and everything else falls into place.

Love for Others

James and I have been blessed in so many ways, and we both love giving back to others. I was able to work with a 501(c)(3) organization called The Something Magic Foundation during my employment with American Airlines. The Something Magic Foundation supports Give Kids The World Village and other children's organizations that fulfill or enhance the wishes of children with life-threatening medical conditions. As an employee of Southwest Airlines, I received an email looking for a volunteer to wear a Santa suit and help with the Spina Bifida Association of North Texas (SBANT) Christmas party. I called James and asked if we could volunteer. We have been the Santa and Mrs. Claus for the SBANT ever since. That is a beautiful way to share love and smiles with children. Our son-in-law created the health and wellness program for a 501(c)(3) organization called The Boot Campaign, which raises funds and awareness for our Veterans. James is on the board of directors, and his favorite time of year with The Boot Campaign is their Santa Boots program. Santa and Mrs. Claus wrap gifts, spread love and cheer, and deliver gifts to local families, while many gifts are shipped out of state.

James has had a life-long love of Corvettes and is fortunate enough to have owned several Corvettes over the last 20 years. James and I are members of the Eureka Springs Corvette Weekend Board of Directors and help to plan and oversee the Corvette Weekend as co-directors of the show.

The saying "Love makes the world go around" is so true. While many would only think of this as romantic love, I believe that we need love in all of its different forms. I can't imagine my life without all the love that I have been blessed with. Having a great family to love and support me, having lifelong friends, finding that special person to be married to, having a family of our own, and—most importantly—the love of God have all shaped my life. Be open to love and share your love with others. May God richly bless you with His divine love.

About Dobby Webb

Dobby was born and raised in North Little Rock, Arkansas, and attended the University of Arkansas at Little Rock. She met and married her college sweetheart, James Webb, and they have two daughters, one son, and now six grandsons. Dobby says, "I am truly blessed with the best family, and their love is my inspiration to keep fighting, no matter what life throws my way."

Dobby was lucky enough to stay at home with her children or to work part-time until they were all in elementary school; then she started working in the school system as a teacher's assistant in special education classes so that she had the same schedule as her children. Once her children started junior high school, she applied at American Airlines and started an 18-year career that included several positions and two cities. Two of her greatest blessings at American Airlines were the wonderful friends that she made there and the volunteer work that she was able to do with the Something mAAgic Foundation, a 501(c)(3) organization where she served as secretary, vice-president, and president of the board of directors. The Something mAAgic Foundation supported a wonderful place called Give Kids The World Village in Orlando, Florida, and various children's organizations by helping to fulfill or enhance the wishes of children with life-threatening medical conditions who want to travel to Orlando, Florida, to visit the local theme parks there. With the merger of American Airlines and US Airways, thousands of employees were laid off, including Dobby. The Something mAAgic Foundation ceased operation due to the pandemic of Covid 19.

Dobby was hired by Southwest Airlines, where she has worked for 10 years. During her 10 years at Southwest Airlines, again she has been blessed with so many special friends who have been so incredibly supportive over the past few years, especially with the health challenges she faced. Another wonderful volunteer opportunity popped up; this time, at Southwest. An email was sent to all of the employees who work at the headquarters, asking for a volunteer to wear a Santa costume for a few hours on a Sunday afternoon for a holiday party for the children of the Spina Bifida Association of North Texas. Dobby called James and asked if they could volunteer … and they have been the SBANT Santa and Mrs. Claus every year since then!

Dobby and James have also volunteered many hours with the Boot Campaign, a 501(c)(3) non-profit corporation whose mission is to unite Americans to honor and restore the lives of veterans and military families through individualized, life-improving programs. While they volunteer in multiple ways, their favorite is the Santa Boots program. Gifts are purchased, wrapped, and delivered to veterans and their families, and James and Dobby are blessed to be Santa and Mrs. Claus for this wonderful program as well. Dobby believes that being able to give back to those who have served our country is an incredible gift.

Dobby and James are both members of the Eureka Springs Corvette Weekend Board of Directors where they help to plan and oversee the Eureka Springs Corvette Weekend as co-directors of the show. (You can check these organizations out at: bootcampaign.org, santaboots.org, gktw.org, spinabifidant.org, and eurekaspringscorvette.org.)

Dobby is a bestselling author as one of the contributing authors to *Mission Hope, Volume II, Stories of Faith and Triumph.* That chapter documents her challenges with breast cancer and a rare autoimmune disease, Chronic Inflammatory Demyelinating Polyneuropathy, which took her from normal movement to being paralyzed from the neck down in just a matter of a few weeks. Her faith in God and her will to fight to overcome these challenges was her salvation.

Closing

So, now, you have read 20 enlightening chapters on the subject of love. From each of these powerful authors' firsthand, true life experiences, they have developed unique and different perspectives and perceptions of love, which now may have moved you to a new place of thinking and understanding more about it. I know, for me, they certainly have.

We have witnessed that love can be seen and heard in a newborn baby's eyes and cries, in the silence of a moment, and in the gift of words whispered, bringing light when we have been in the dark and the knowing that someone special walks beside us, even if we're not in their physical or spiritual realm. We have witnessed the love of Spirit that lives within each one of us. Love is real and tangible.

It's interesting to note the various similarities, as well as the differences, between these beautiful love stories. From how they first discovered love to how they view it now, how it feels, and even how it tastes to them. Every one of these courageous authors has come from different backgrounds and perspectives. Most have come to their conclusions through serious pain, illness, and heartbreak to discover more self-love, self-awareness, empathy, caring, and compassion. They did it through hope and faith, delving deep into their soul's heart space to uncover more meaning in their lives. Some have sadly lost love and loved ones and reported back that they found this journey to tell their stories through love to be very cathartic and healing. They now have a better understanding of themselves, those they interacted with before, as well as those they interact with now.

We hope that you, dear reader, also have a better understanding and more clarity on the true meaning of love and how it relates and translates to your life path. Could you identify with our stories? How did they make you feel? Were you surprised to learn something you can use to move forward with more love in your life? Do you believe that love heals the heartbroken, downhearted, and even the sick? Do you believe that love can heal and transform our hurting world? We certainly do because we have seen it happen in our own lives—miracles of healing right before our very eyes. It's akin to the domino effect, as each of us is connected to a higher consciousness, the One who breathed love and life into us. We are here to serve, learn, grow, and make a bigger impact together, each one a spark of the Divine. If God is love, then we are all love as well. What happens to one ultimately affects us all. Love can and will heal our world. Maybe not in our lifetime, but what about in the lives of our grandchildren, great-grandchildren, and great-grandchildren's children? This book is our legacy and gift to the world. Pass it on so that those who come after us will have a point of reference for how we lived our lives.

Is love that difficult now for you? Are you still questioning how, why, or what? If so, we are here to help you through the unraveling process, and it is a process, my friends. We are the helpers; it is our purpose in life. Not to say any of us has all the answers yet, or if we ever will, but we who have been where you are now are always open to giving you hope and the faith to persevere. Hang on through the maze of love and find fulfillment with more grace, joy, and gratitude in life. These are the hinge pins life clings to. We have three more of these anthologies to write, and those are the very things we will be writing about next. Many of these brilliant authors will visit us again. We hope you will read all of our books.

Thank you for being here, experiencing for yourself through our stories what love means to us. Take whatever you have learned here and go help us change the world! If you are interested in joining our mission of hope, please reach out to me or one of our authors. Love, hope, and faith change everything. Regardless, we would love to hear from you.

Remember this: love never dies; love never ends; love is kindness; love is service to mankind; love is empowering; and love is eternal. With hope, faith, and love, anything is possible. And if you believe and trust in your heart, then miracles happen. However you serve it up, go share some love and kindness today and every day. We love you!

And to wrap it all up, as one of our dear authors Maria Lehtman says, "Love is the bridge between our souls. Love is all."

Namaste,

Char Murphy, Visionary, creator, and curator of Mission Hope and the Mission Hope anthology book series

www.ourmissionhope.com

About Char Murphy

 Char is a heart-driven servant leader, successful attorney, entrepreneur, and multi-award-winning best-selling author. As a person who deeply cares about others' success, and being a source of inspiration, she has been recognized as an expert for her ability to write inspiring books using her story of overcoming breast cancer four different times. She uses this amazing story to uplift and encourage others going through serious life-altering circumstances and challenges to realize they are stronger, more capable, more courageous, and better equipped to withstand and heal from any hardship than they may think. She believes wholeheartedly, "If I can do it, you can do it too."

Char's current long-term passion project is Mission Hope, consisting of a best-selling anthology book series comprising collaborative stories about overcoming and healing from serious adversities and loss through hope, faith, love, grace, joy, and gratitude. This mission was divinely inspired and born when she was guided through meditation by God (or Spirit) to bring like-minded souls together to write their personal stories on these subjects and publish the books. Again, to uplift, encourage, and let the readers know they're not alone in their struggles. One of Char's favorite quotes is, "Always look for the gift in everything, even the perceived not-so-good." She feels blessed and grateful to still be alive, sharing her gifts and stories with the world to inspire and give hope to others. Char says, "Breast cancer saved my life so I can fully live my passion and purpose."

She has coached and helped dozens of people write their stories in books. She gives all the credit to God and her brave and passionate authors for the great success of these books. We are grateful to you, our dear reader, for supporting our shared mission to make the world a better place for all to live and thrive together.

If you are interested in writing your story of healing and overcoming serious adversity to inspire others, please contact Char Murphy to submit a writing sample. Thank you.

Email: char@ourmissionhope.com
Website: www.ourmissionhope.com

Works of Interest

Unshakeable Power - Thriving Through Seasons of the Soul

A memoir of Char's life growing up. From a childhood of abuse to losing her father to ALS when she was only 24 years old—she was his only caretaker at home as a single mom of a two-year-old child. Then, at the age of 32, she went back to school to get her law degree. She practiced law for 15 years and had a very successful law practice of her own until breast cancer reared its ugly head not once but four different times. Her doctors told her that if she didn't quit practicing law, the stress was going to kill her.

The book goes on from there to tell how she handled a total change of lifestyle and lost everything, including her home and her then-husband. She calls herself a "breast cancer thriver," not just a survivor.

Char knows quite well what it's like to go through and overcome serious adversity with back-to-back experiences. This book is loaded with valuable inspiration and the tools needed to help readers know that they, too, can overcome serious life-altering circumstances. In her own words, "It takes a strong will to survive and thrive when all the chips are down; a strength you didn't know you had, which has been there all along. This kind of perseverance isn't rare or hard to find. You just have to reach down deep enough inside to access it and then use it to become the best version of you yet." She says, "Don't ever give up. Just believe in yourself; have hope and faith; embrace love with grace and gratitude and keep going. Miracles do happen every day."

Her readers say: "A must-read book about a lifetime of grit and determination, the perseverance to rise and conquer it all with hope, faith, love, grace, and gratitude."

Mission Hope, Volume I

This collection of personal and professional stories is written from the heart by everyday people just like you. They will make you laugh and make you cry. Above all, it will give you more confidence and strength to confront your own adversities in life and to know you're not alone.

The authors of *Mission Hope* have been where you are right now. They want you to know that if they can go through it and come out better, more empowered, and on the other side of what feels like a total disaster, you can do it too. A new season of hope is coming soon.

Mission Hope, Volume II

Life's many upheavals, sharp curves, twists and turns, the challenging circumstances coming right at you are non-stop. The inner wars within and outside your control feel overwhelming; you feel alone, and the seemingly endless battles rage on. You feel like you have lost all hope and faith, questioning, *Why me? Why now? How can I handle another blow?*

The answers you're seeking are in this collection of 20 uplifting stories, in this book, right here in your hands. Within its golden pages, from the deep confines of their hearts and souls, these extraordinary authors have opened up and are here to assist you in navigating the deep, daunting, dark waters you are facing.

Each story is unique in its experience but similar in the fact that through everything presented to them in life, they found the way back to success, peace, and joy through hope and faith. They turned tragedy into tranquility once again. Now, they are here to empower you to shift from what once was fear and failure into the future of your dreams. They offer as a gift to you the freedom to choose your destiny. Now, it's time to turn the key and walk through the doors. See you on the other side!